OUT TO THE BALL GAME

with Tom Wolfe

Text Written with and
Photography by
Douglas Congdon-Martin

Schiffer Publishing Ltd
77 Lower Valley Road, Atglen, PA 19310

Published by Schiffer Publishing, Ltd.
77 Lower Valley Road
Atglen, PA 19310
Please write for a free catalog.
This book may be purchased from the publisher.
Please include $2.95 postage.
Try your bookstore first.

We are interested in hearing from authors
with book ideas on related subjects.

Copyright © 1992 by Thomas Wolfe.
Library of Congress Catalog Number: 92-63110.

All rights reserved. No part of this work may be reproduced or used in any forms or by any means—graphic, electronic or mechanical, including photocopying or information storage and retrieval systems—without written permission from the copyright holder.

Printed in the United States of America.
ISBN: 0-88740-497-9

Contents

Introduction

I don't know what it is about baseball that gets under people's skins like it does. Maybe it's the combination of team work and individual effort. Maybe it's the tradition of 150 years...America's first homegrown sport. Maybe it's the peanuts and Cracker Jacks. Whatever it is baseball continues to fascinate young and old alike.

One thing that's certain is that baseball has always had its share of colorful characters. In the early years there was Asa Brainard, the great picture who intimidated batters with his mutton-chop side whiskers. A little later Cap Anson dominated the game with his feisty personality, and Mike "King" Kelly thrilled the crowds in Boston. Then came John McGraw and the powerful New York Giants, Ty Cobb in Detroit, Babe Ruth of the Yankees. Each generation had produced heroes whose names have a familiar ring. Joe DiMaggio, Ted Williams, Yogi Berra, Mickey Mantle, Casey Stengel. Even an umpire like Bill Klem, who "never" made a bad call has found his way into the Hall of Fame.

I like the images they evoke in me, and the figures in this book try to capture some of the character of the game and of its heroes. The cocky young pitcher. The rotund manager. The stiff umpire. The batter going into battle.

I hope you enjoy carving these ballplayers as much as I did. Please use your own favorite team's uniform, and maybe you can try to shape the face into a portrait of your own personal hero.

The Tools and Patterns

The tools needed for this project include a simple set of palm gouges, a turned-down blade and a turned-up blade, and some eye punches or nailsets for the eyes and buttons. The wood I use is bass, and it is probably the best for these figures. It carves and takes the paint nicely.

The patterns are reproduced at their actual size as indicated with each pattern. You may use them as they appear or enlarge or reduce them on a photo-copying machine. While you are at the copying machine, print several copies so you can cut them apart as needed to help in the drawing of the various parts.

I do not use a full-frontal pattern because I find it leads to more trouble than its worth. People tend to try to follow it too exactly and find that at some point they have cut off something they're going to need later. Besides, if everything is laid out too completely it limits the creativity that comes in the carving. The photographs in the book are designed to give plenty of guidance without overdoing it. I have included full-size frontal photographs of each figure so you can use it as an accurate guide.

The Pitcher

Mickey "Knuckles" O'Toole

Carving the Pitcher

Cut the pattern from a piece of bass about 4″ thick. I use a four inch piece for every thing I carve. Of course you can do the same thing with a two inch piece and the pattern shrunk in half. In any case I'd rather use a piece that is too wide than one that is too skinny.

Find the center of the blank and mark it. Carry the line all the way around.

With a coping saw or a band saw I will split the legs up to the crotch.

Choose which leg is to be forward and...

at the same time, mark the arm that is to be back.

Mark the area to be removed behind the forward arm.

On the head blank draw in the neck and mark the area to be removed.

I drill off the leg and arm areas to be removed with a drill press. This gives me speed, but a gouge chisel will do as well.

The neck hole should be just a little smaller than the diameter of the neck.

Begin by carving the neck square.

Then cut the corners off into an octagon.

Try a test fit. For now we leave the neck long. It acts as a nice handle while we carve the head.

Mark around the hat band...

and the return of the bill.

Make a stop along the bill line by putting pressure on the back of the knife and rocking back and forth.

Cut back to the stop from corners of the face. This creates an octagon. Going to the octagon shape before going to round seems to help give the piece a better look.

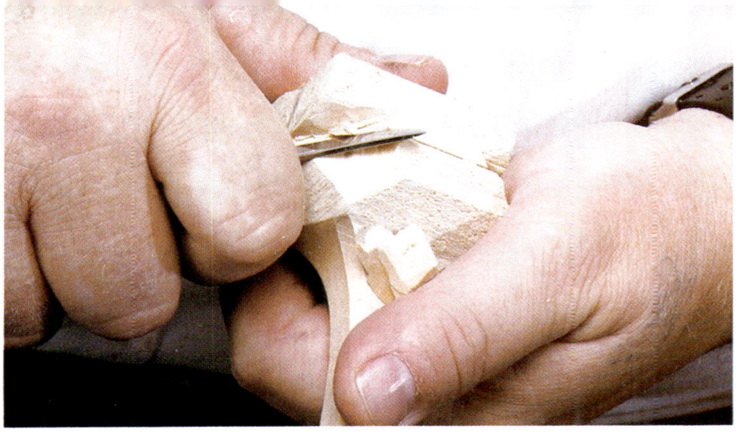

Continue to knock off the corners the full length of the face.

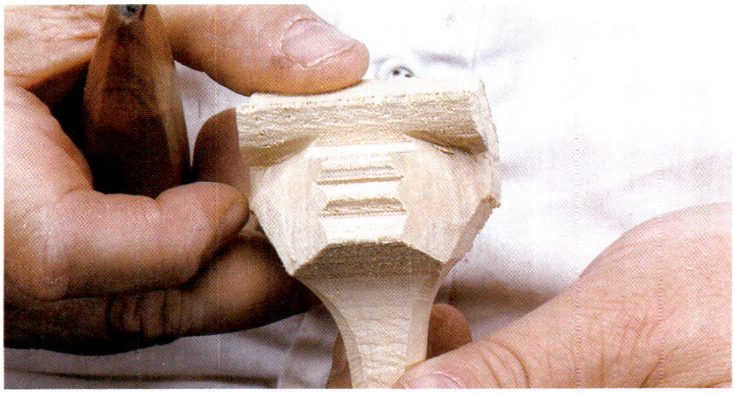

This brings the face to this state.

Knock off the back corners of the head.

With the long handled knife I get good leverage and power. The thumb of the holding hand acts as a fulcrum on which the knife turns.

Starting above the ear line, trim the top of the carving. This narrows the cap, but leaves wood at the ears in case you want to leave them comically big.

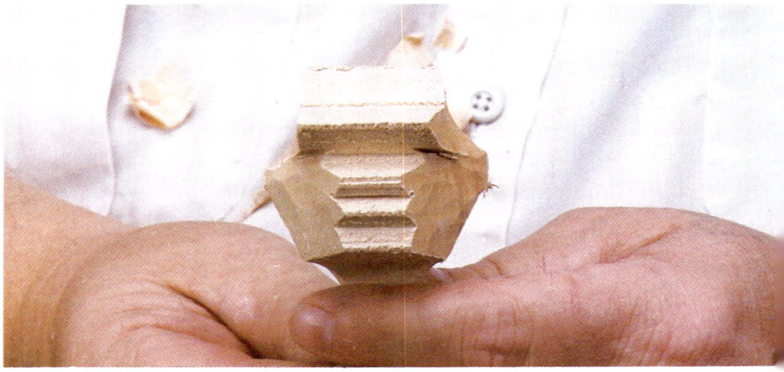

Progress report.

With a gouge chisel come up under the bill. I do it now because there is still a lot of stock around to support it. Don't try to get the bill too thin or it will break. Draw the line of the curve of the bill.

Find a gouge that will match the sweep of the line. Push straight in with the gouge at the thickness of the bill. Be careful not to undercut it. This creates a stop under the bill.

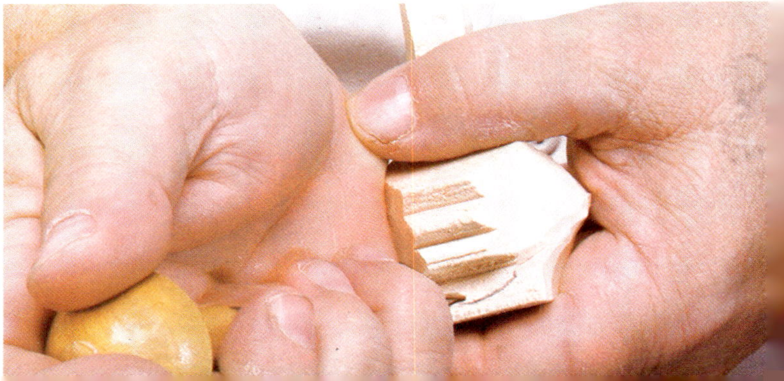

Go back with a knife and clean out the area under the bill. Use a knife that is turned down or flat on the blade. Cut back to the stop.

This should take you about to this point.

Round the bill by knocking off the corners.

Slope the top of the bill back to the cap.

Carry a center line from the neck through the face.

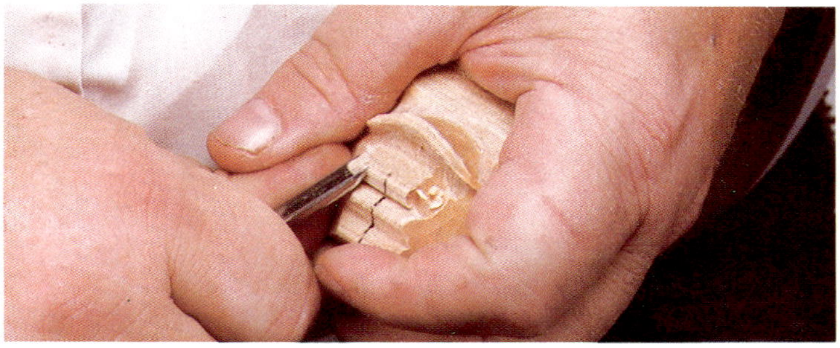

Use a small half round chisel to remove the cheek area beside the nose. Leave plenty of nose for now.

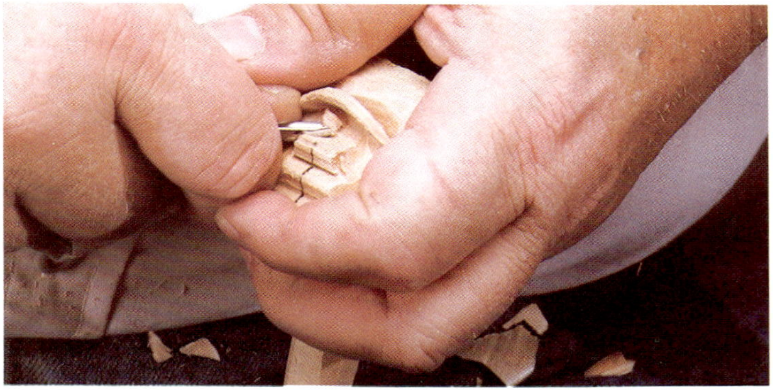

Carry the line up to the bridge of the nose, leaving the nose triangular shaped.

Deepen the cut a little to form the eyesocket.

With a knife round the end of the nose to a nice button shape.

On the sides of the nose cut in with a 45 degree cut for the nostril.

Come back to it from the lip and pop it off.

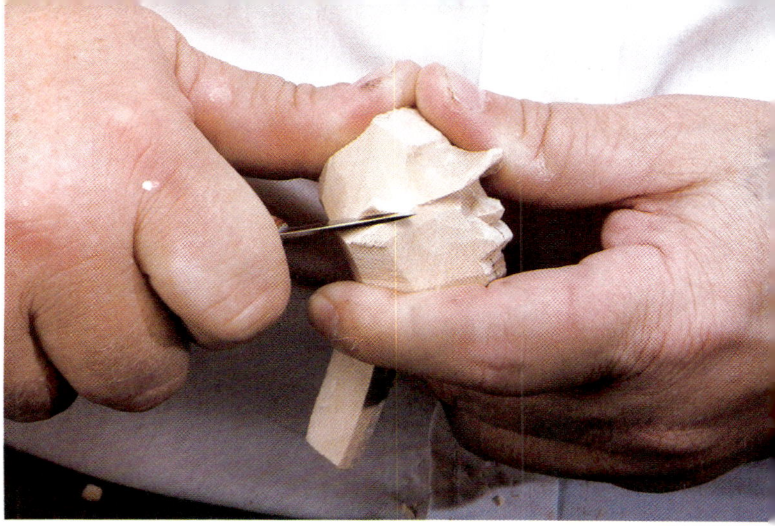

Define the bottom edge of the cap. Start by trimming a little off the top of the ear. You want the ear to come over the bottom of the cap, but not too far.

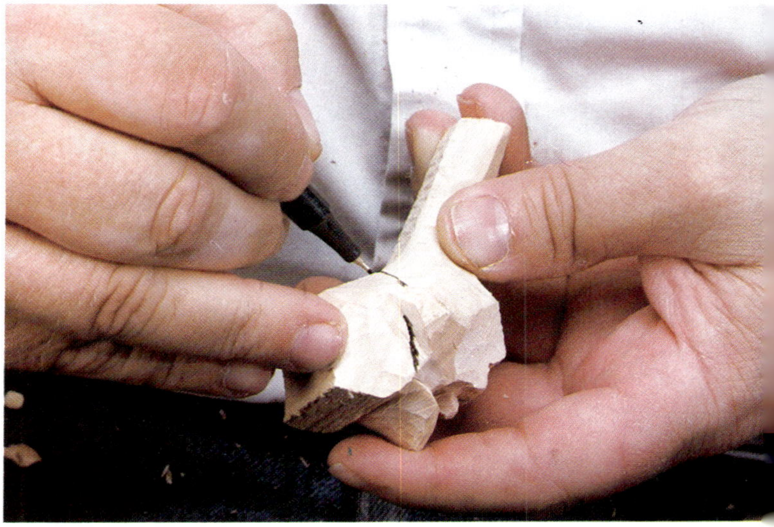

Draw in the bottom of the cap.

The top of the ear is pretty much defined already, even with the eyes. Mark the bottom of the ear even with the bottom of the nose.

The front of the ear is in line with the jaw.

Square off the ear.

Trim all around the ear, cutting into the line for a stop...

and back to it from the head.

This leaves a boxy ear, that can be shaped later.

Cut a stop around the bottom edge of the cap.

Carve back to the stop from the hair.

Round off the cap, taking away everything that doesn't look like a baseball cap.

The cap rounded off.

Come from under the ear with a gouge to define the chin line and the base of the skull.

Clean the area with a knife.

With a pointed knife cut straight in beside the nose

Cut a stop along the cheek line...

and carve back to it from the lip.

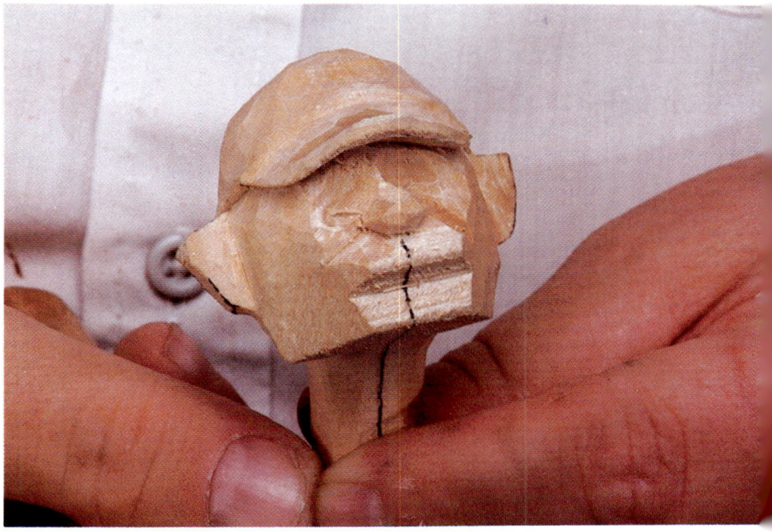

This defines the bottom of the cheek and the top of the moustache.

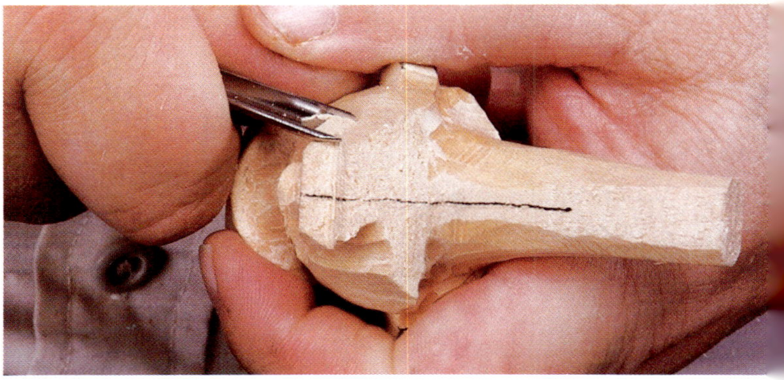

Carry the cheek line down to the chin using a gouge.

This brings out the chin.

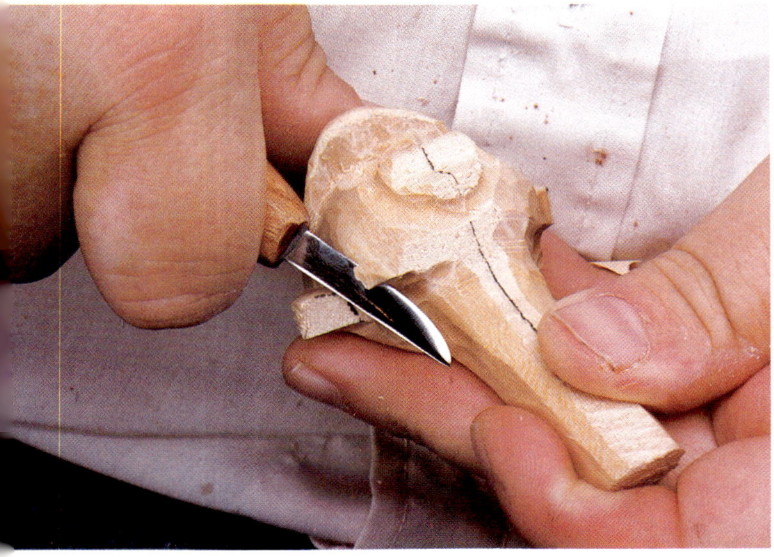

Round off the jaw and bring it to the chin.

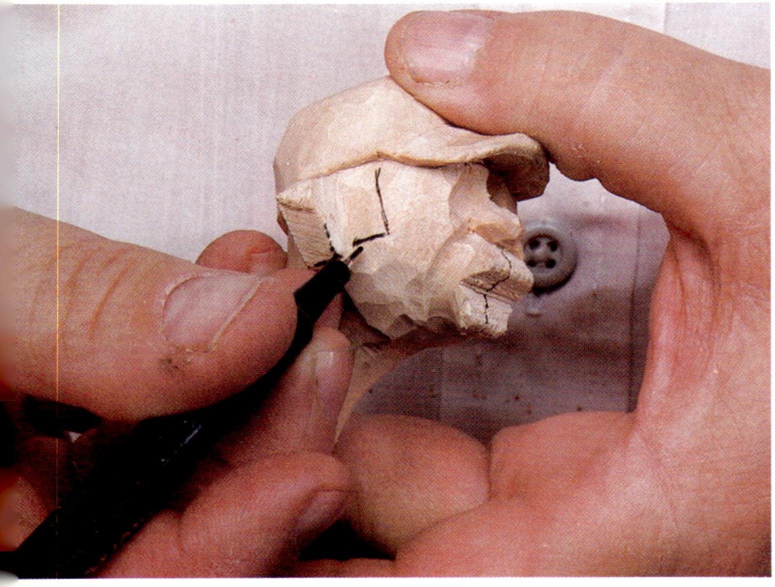

Draw in the sideburns. The ears should be further than half way back, giving plenty of room for the sideburns.

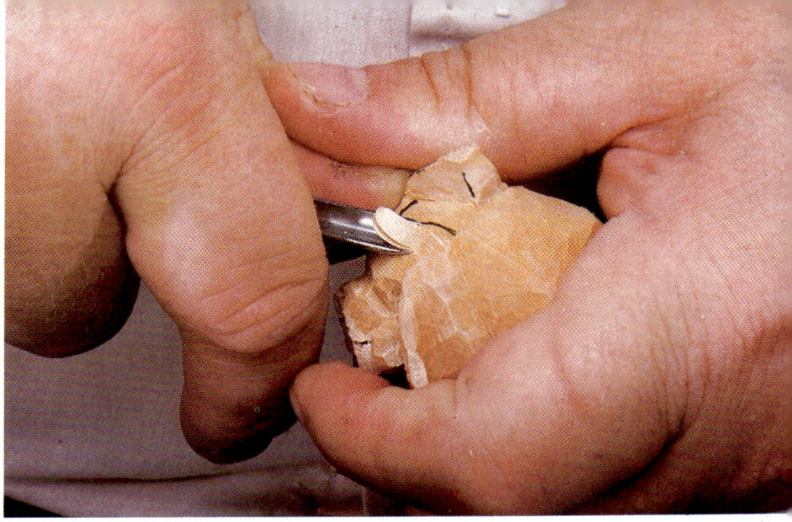

Cut up the front edge of the sideburn with a gouge. Notice the position of the thumbs. This acts as a check against cutting too far and going into the cap. The forefinger of the knife hand also acts as a stop, keeping you from going too far.

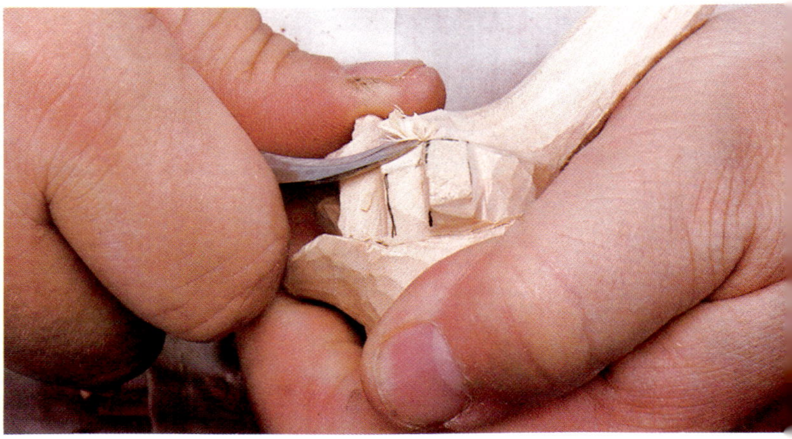

Cut down at the bottom of the sideburn and pop off the excess.

Progress.

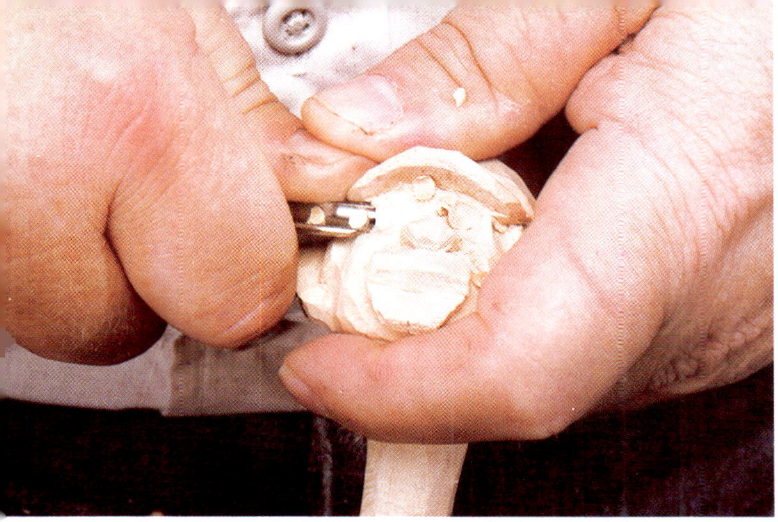

With a gouge, come from the temple into the eyesocket, blending the two. This also helps define the cheek.

With a small half-round gouge come in under the nose to form the nostril.

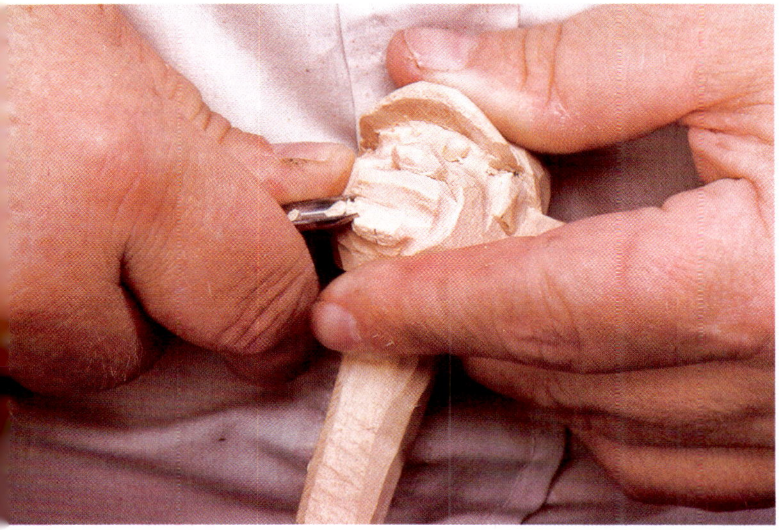

With the chisel, come across the chin under the bottom lip.

Pick the piece out of the nostril using a pointed knife.

Round the chin itself with a knife.

Come over the top of the nostril with the gouge with the cup out.

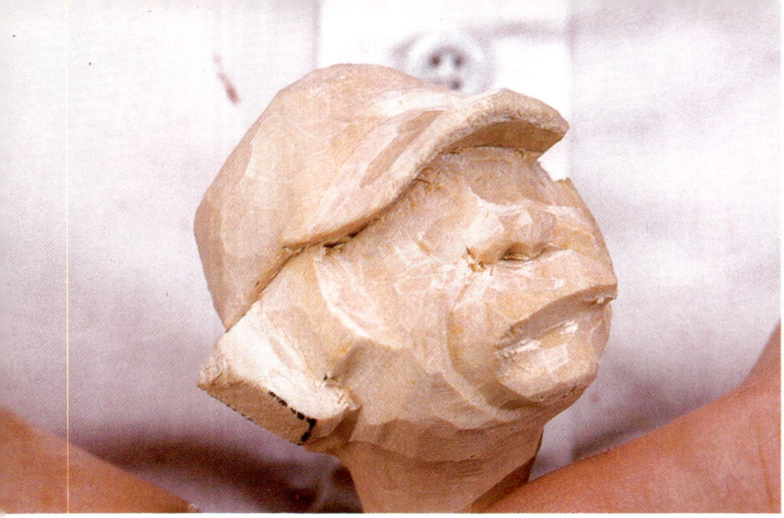

The shaped nose.

This leaves a little lower lip.

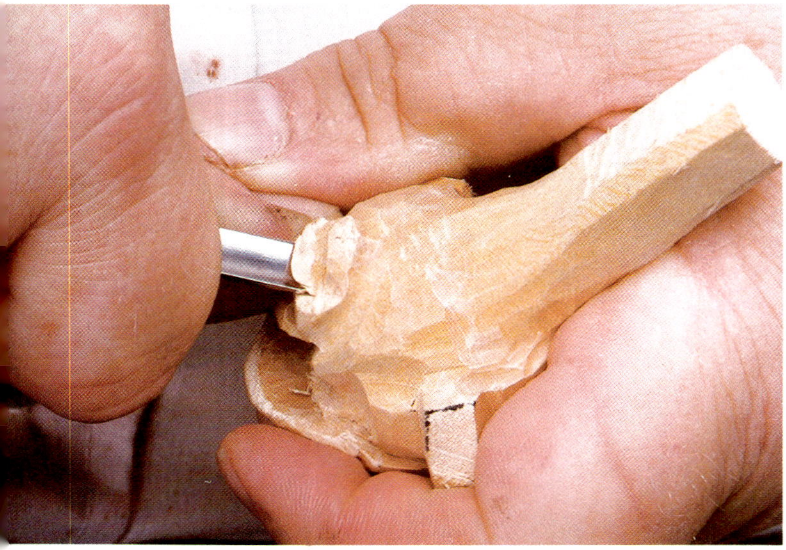

Come into the bottom of the moustache with a flatter gouge.

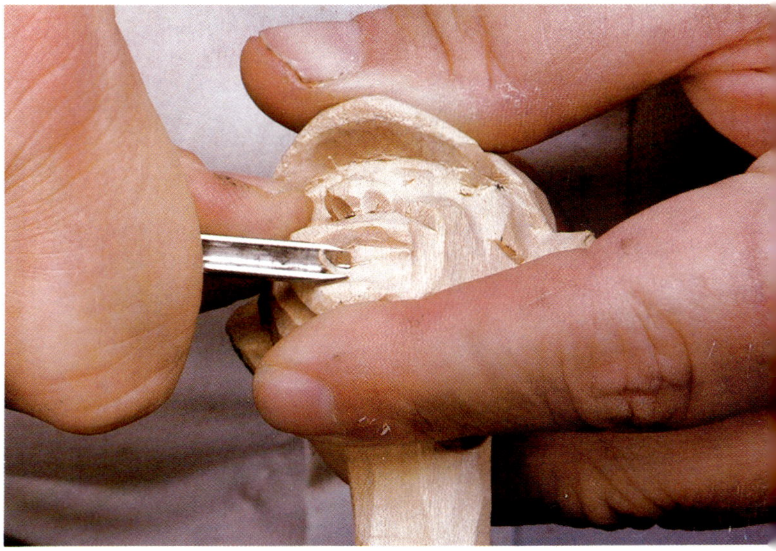

With a small U-shaped gouge go across the underside of the bottom lip to bring it out more.

Carve back to it with a knife, leaving enough for the bottom lip.

To define the moustache cut a stop down the cheek line...

and trim back to it from the moustache.

The face is taking on character.

Returning to the ears, slant the outer surface back.

Shape the outer edge of the ears. When moving to the other ear, hold the piece for a good perspective. You want the size and angle to be pretty close.

Cut a stop along the back edge of the sideburn.

With a gouge, start about half way into the ear and cut a cup toward the stop. First do a small one in the lower half of the ear...

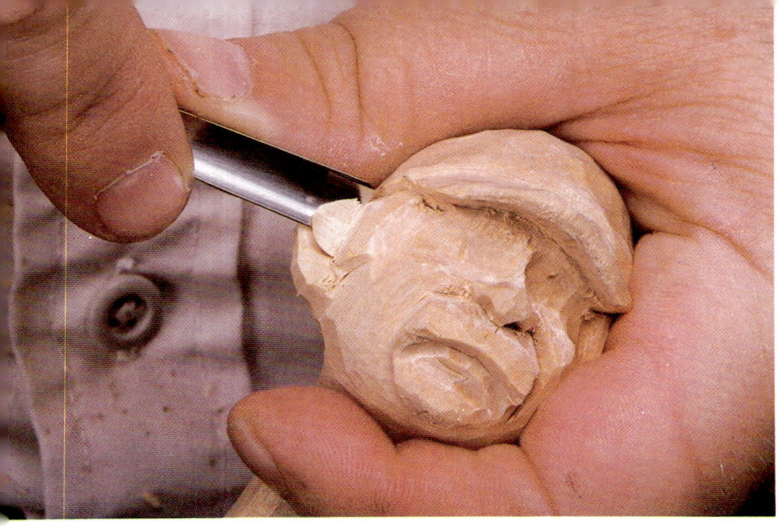

Then do a small one in the upper half. If you try to do one large cup, you are likely to bust the ear off.

With the veiner create the detail on the inside of the ear. Be careful not to go against the grain, at either end of the ear, or you will bust if off. Work toward the center.

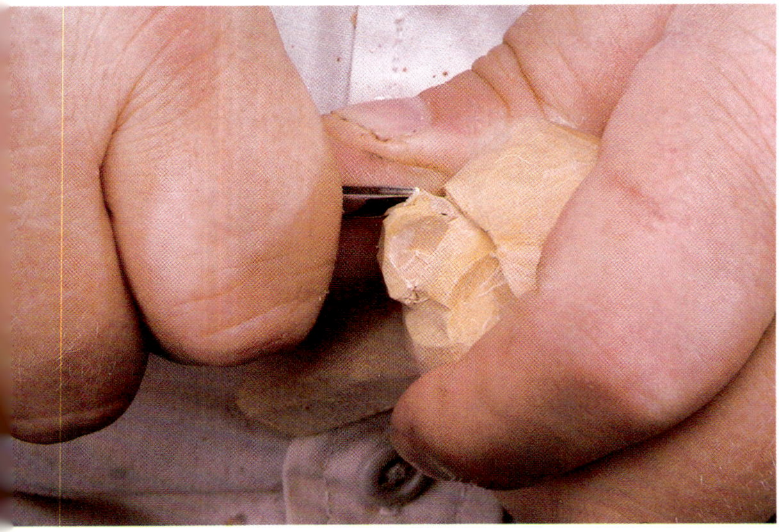

When the cup of the ear is established, use a small U-shaped gouge to go behind the ear, defining its thickness. Just go in a little bit.

The finished ears.

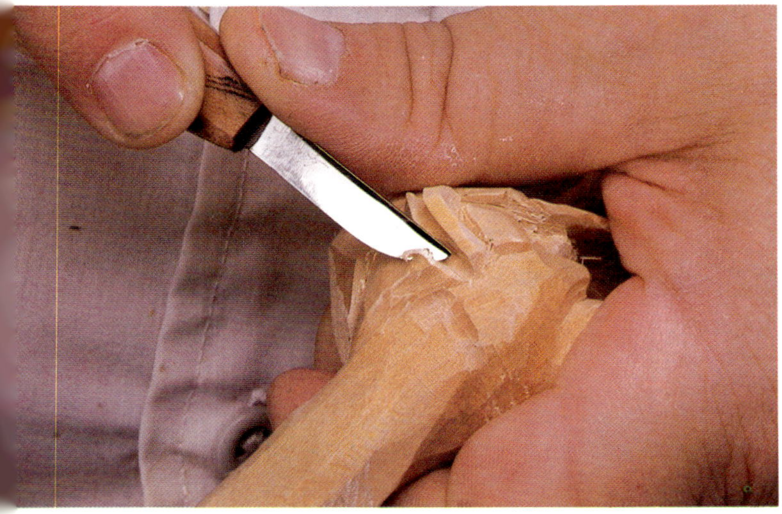

Round off the bottom of the back of the ear, where the ear joins the head. With prominent ears like this, you need to pay attention to detail.

After cleaning up some saw marks it is time to fit the head to the body. The eyes, hairline, and other details will wait. Bevel the edge around the neck hole. this will make it look like the collar is rolled around his neck, and not straight up.

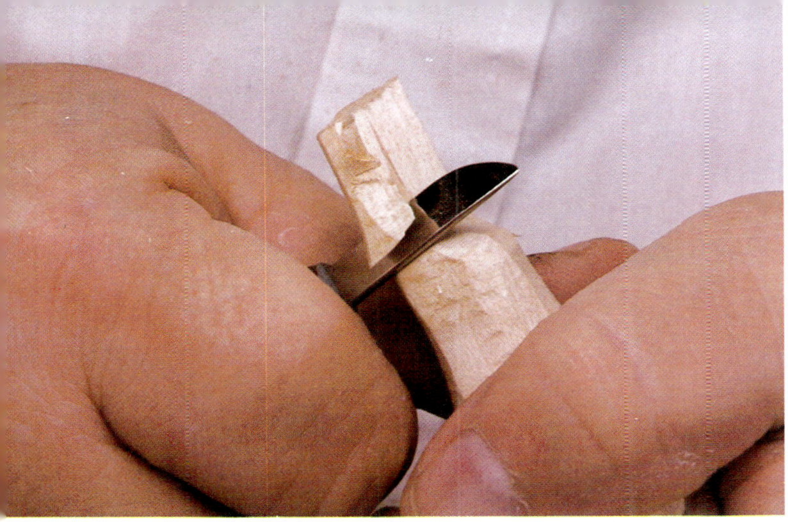

At this point the neck is way too long, so we just shave off the end of it.

Put the head in the hole and twist it back and forth while applying pressure. By doing this the high spots will get shiny, so...

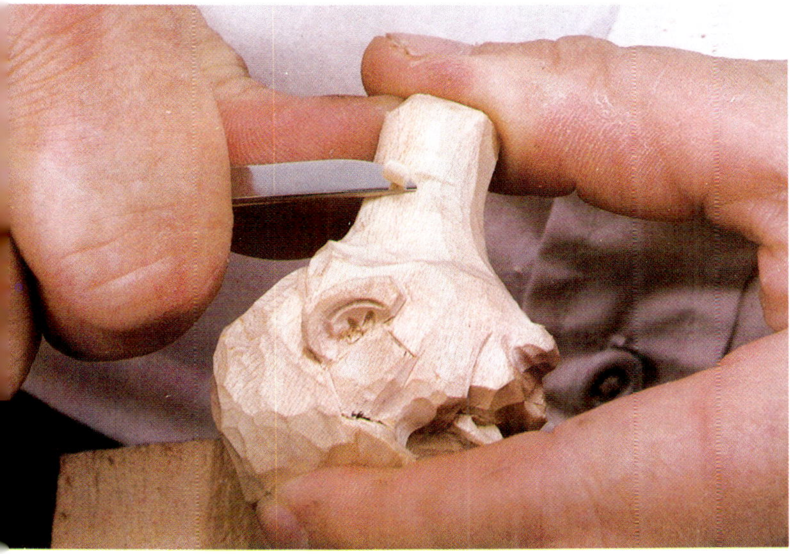

when you take it out you will be able to see where to trim.

With the head fitted, you can see that the body will have to be reduced quite a bit to be proportional.

The darkened areas will have to be removed. This needs to be removed by hand, because if you try to use a bandsaw, you will probably lose an arm (the player's, not yours!!).

More darkened areas that need to be removed.

Cut away the excess using a knife or gouge, depending on which works best.

Use a flatter gouge to clean up the lines left by the drill press.

The front foot will point out at a rather severe angle. Mark the sole.

The rear foot will also point out, but not so much. Mark it too.

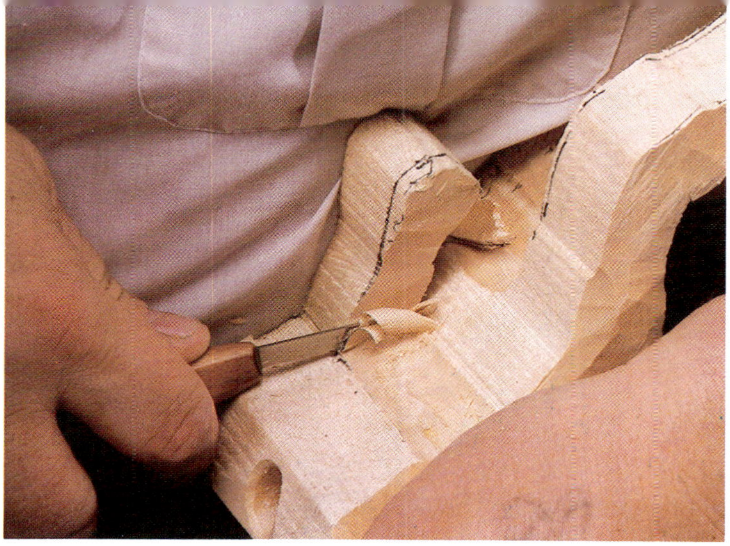

Clean the inside of the forward arm.

Trim away the excess on the other side.

Clean the excess beside the foot. It is with the grain, so it should just pop off.

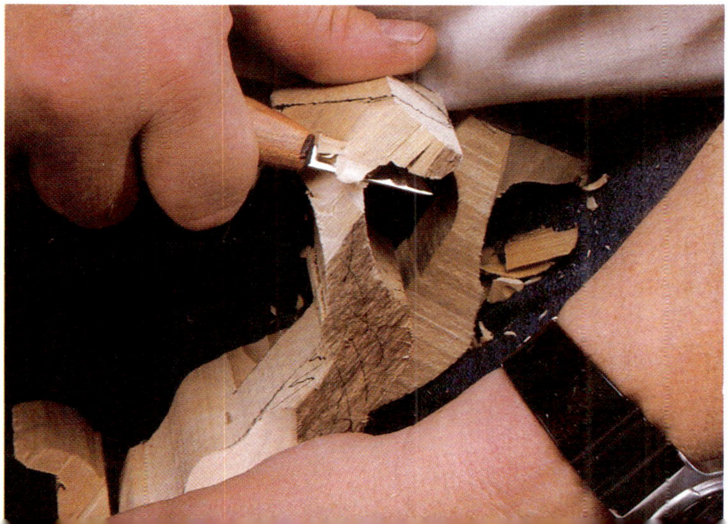

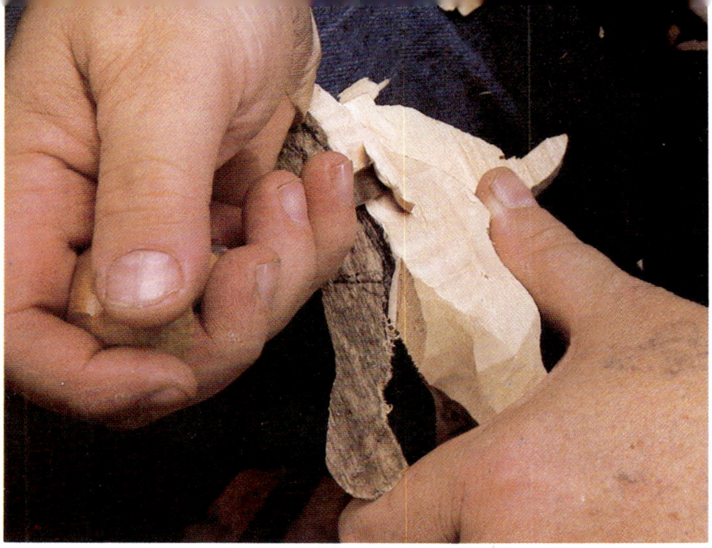

With a sweeping motion, use the gouge to remove the area behind the forward arm.

Use the knife to round off the back and hips.

The glove will be at an angle like this, which gives it its maximum size.

Knock out the overall shape of the glove.

Begin to round the arm over.

The shoulder of the right arm needs to come back with the line continuing to the elbow and then turning toward the wrist. Mark it in. In the pattern the arm looks short, but with this angle it is much longer than the pattern appears to make it.

This roughs in the back arm.

Trim the arm to the line.

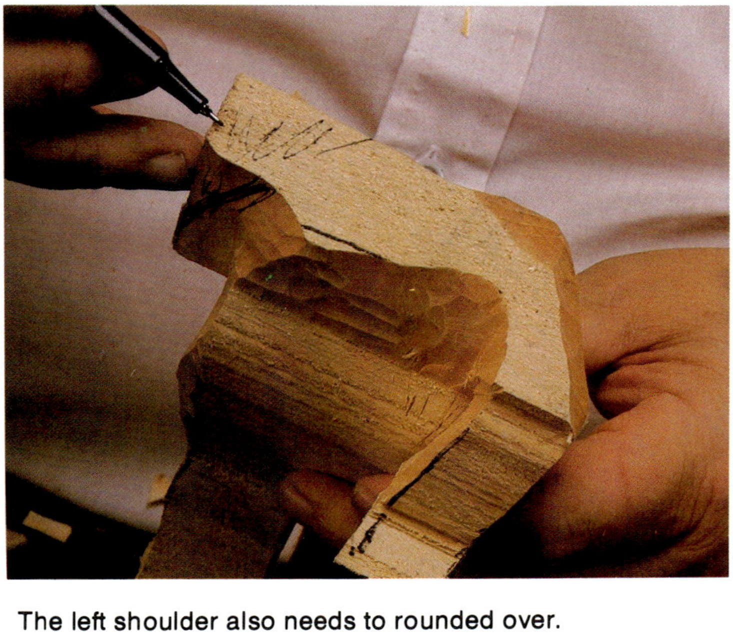

The left shoulder also needs to rounded over.

Continue to round the back.

With the elbow set, we can carve the inside of the arm so that it looks right, gradually coming out away from the body. The elbow is an important reference point.

It helps to draw in the line of the back of the arm. This gets the elbow in the proper place.

Cut a stop between the arm and the body.

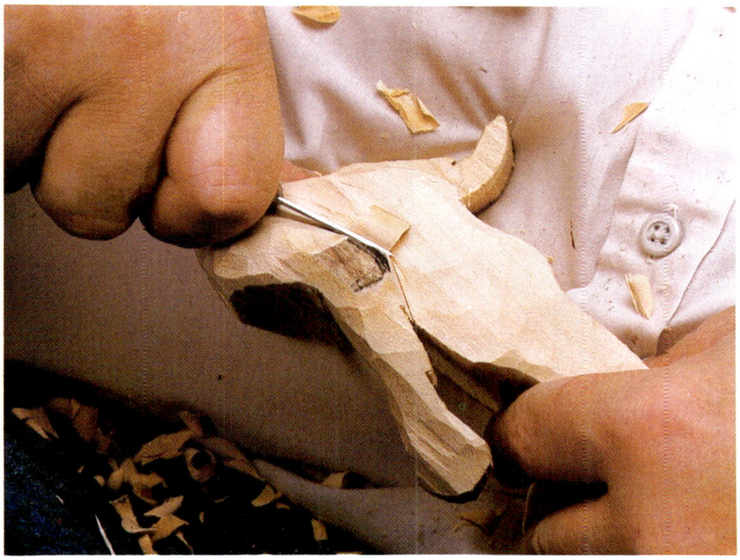

Trim back to the line.

Trim back to the stop from the chest.

Make a stop at the bottom of the sleeve.

This upper forearm is still a little thick on the inside, so I mark the area to be trimmed.

Trim back to the stop from the forearm.

The glove arm is taking shape.

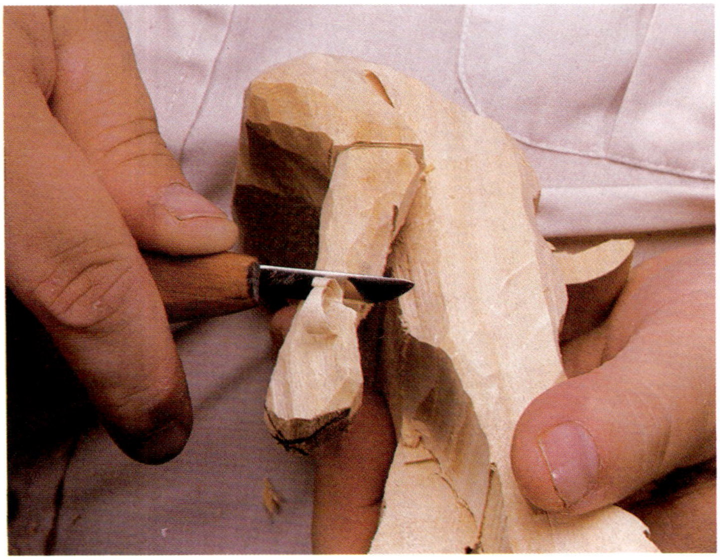

Round the forearm down. Don't go too far until you've decided where the glove will be.

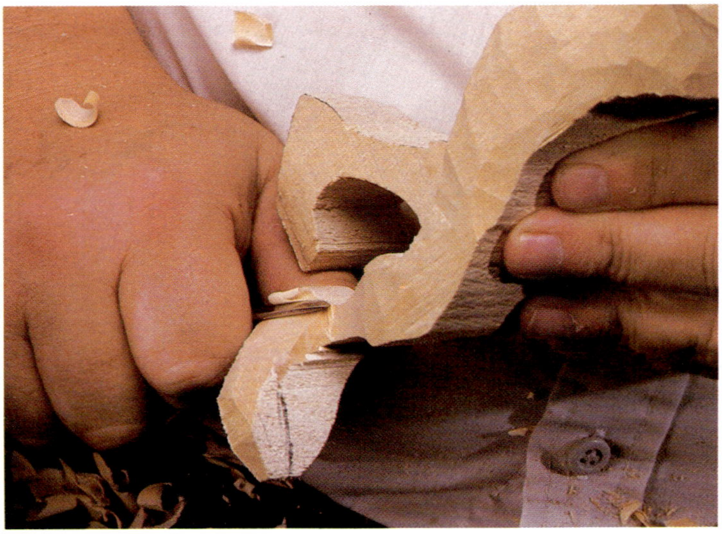

We shift our attention to the legs. I start by narrowing the ankles, because that's where you get messed up. You don't want to make them flat.

Begin by squaring them off until the overall thickness is the right size. Keep a good blouse at the end of the trousers.

Round the lower legs off by going first to octagonal...

Mark the top of the shoe. This should not be at the narrowest part of the ankle, but where the ankle starts flaring out again.

then to round.

Follow the shoe line with a veiner.

Repeat the process on the back foot and leg.

The lower legs take shape.

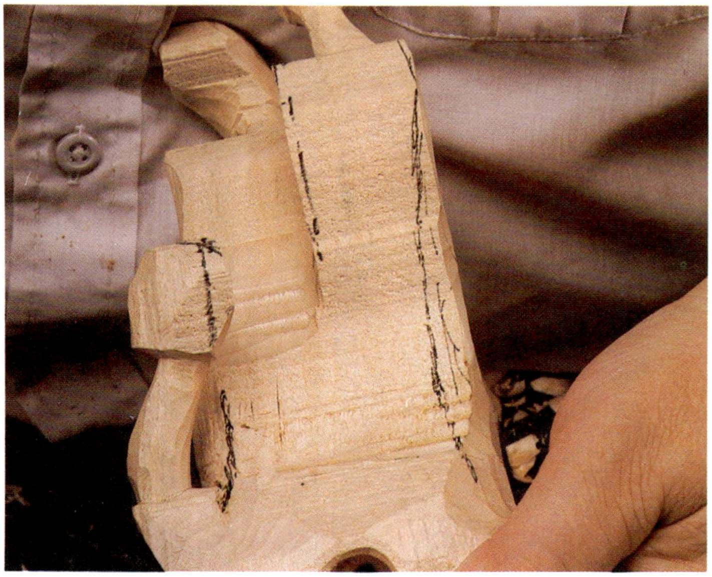

The figure needs thinning. Mark the area to be removed.

Mark it front and back.

Trim the sides to square.

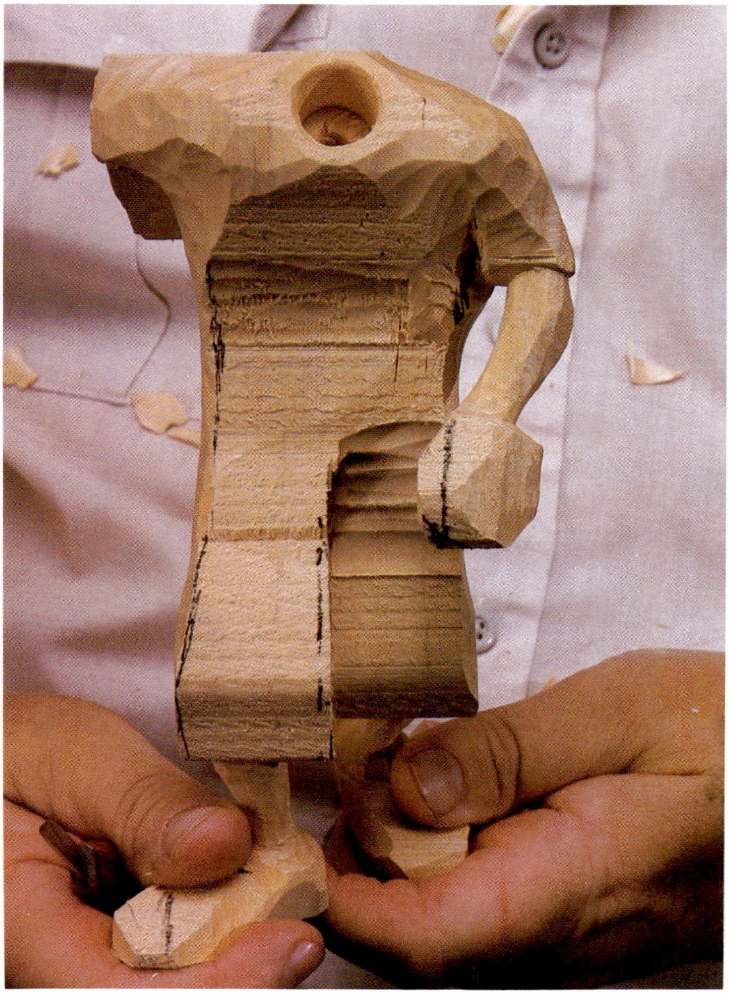

The sides are narrower and square.

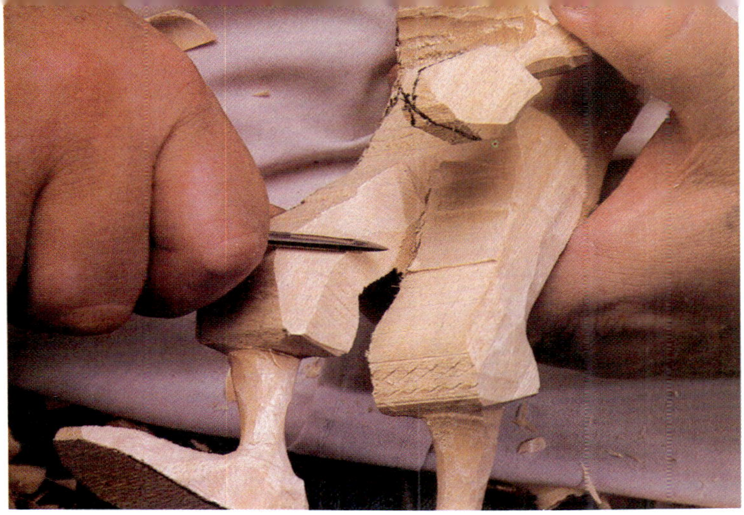

Knock off the corners of the legs all around.

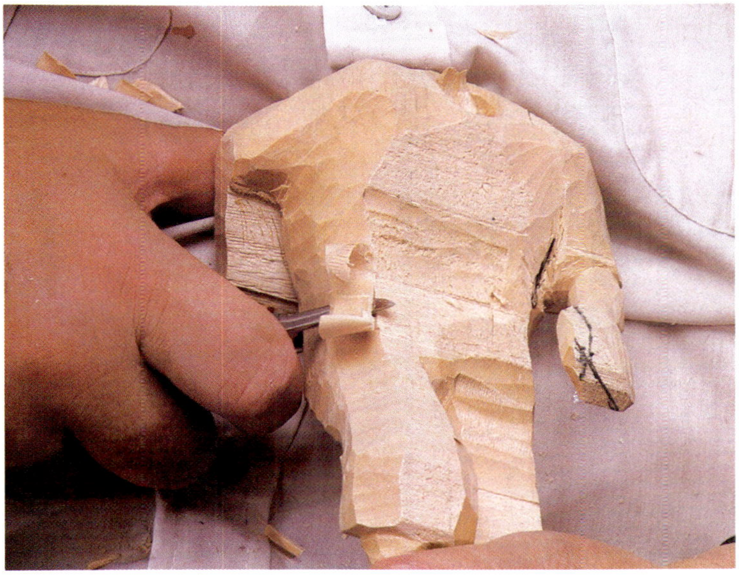

Continue up the chest.

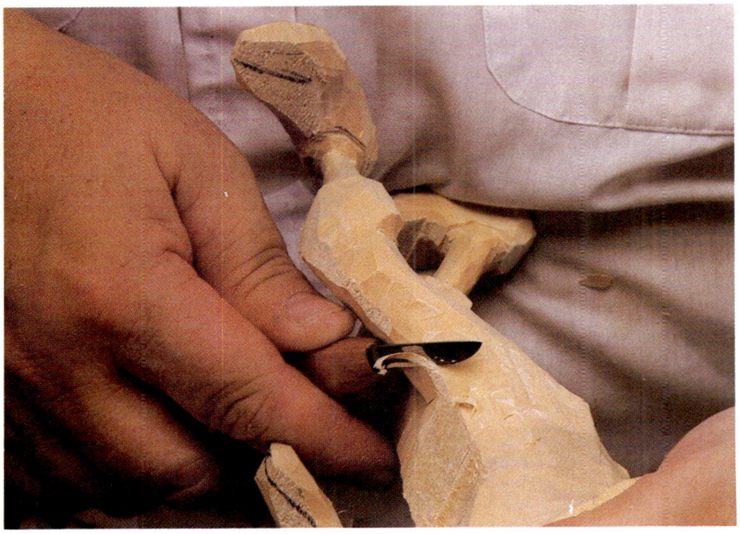

Round up the legs. On this player the legs were looking a little flat, so to get the proper shape I have to "skinny them up" a bit.

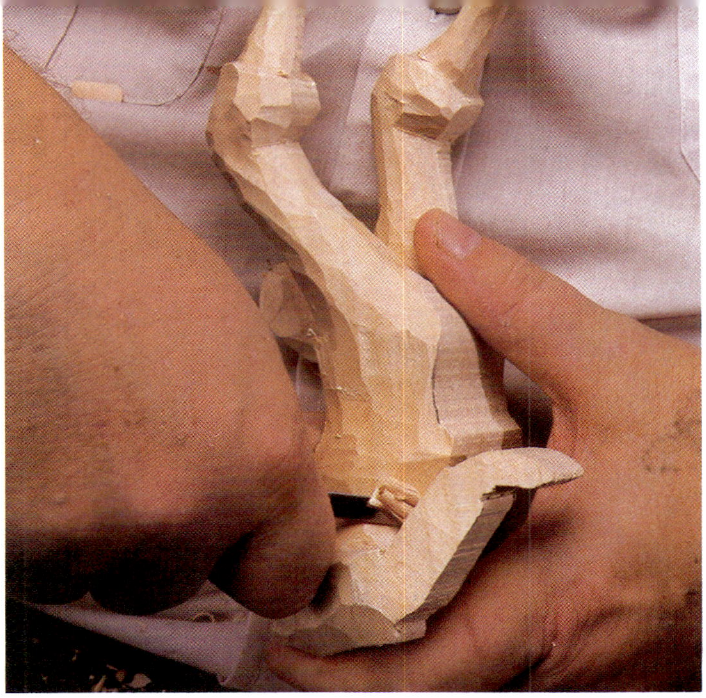

With the thinner legs, I need to narrow the upper body too.

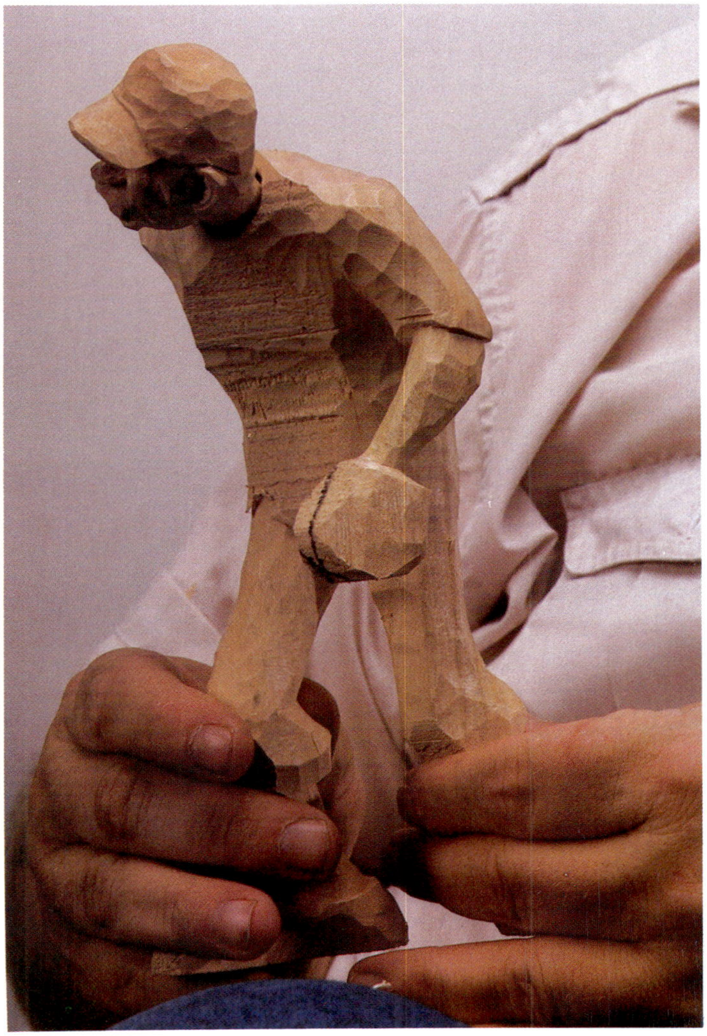

The front is taking on some good shape.

The back is left blousey for now.

Trim the forearm to the wrist.

Knock off the corners of the back.

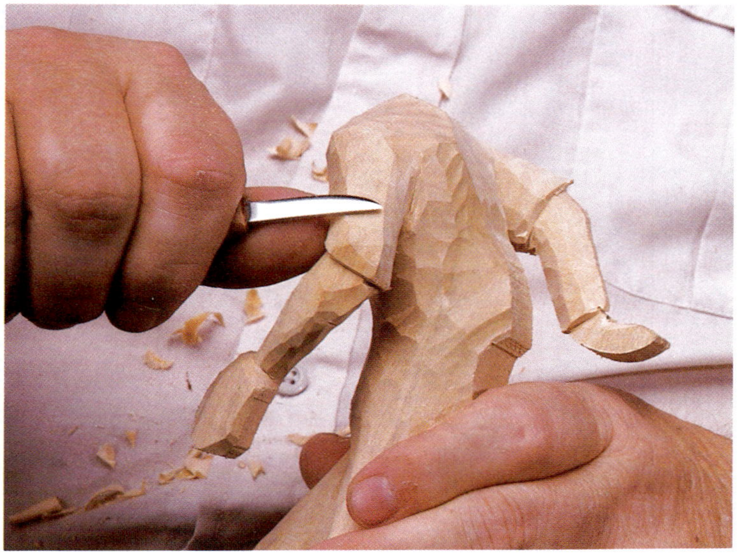

Knock the corners off to bring the forearm to round.

Thin the wrist above the back hand. Again keep things square until you get to the diameter you seek.

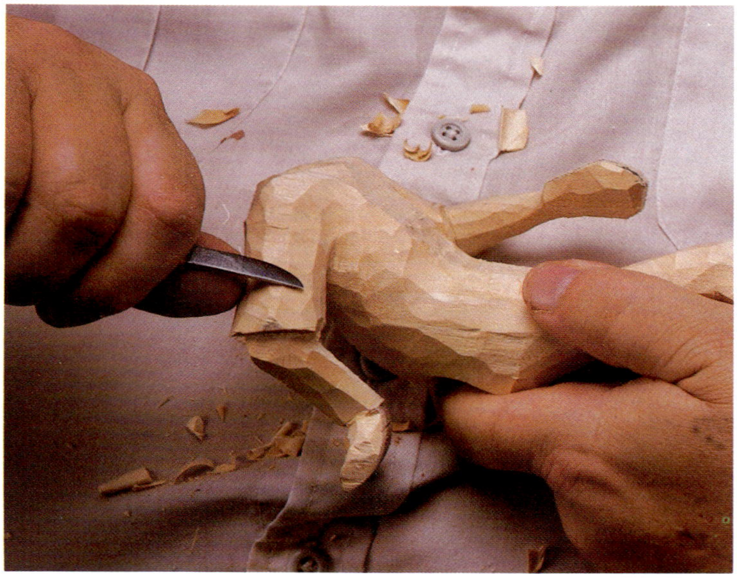

The front arm is much thinner than the back...

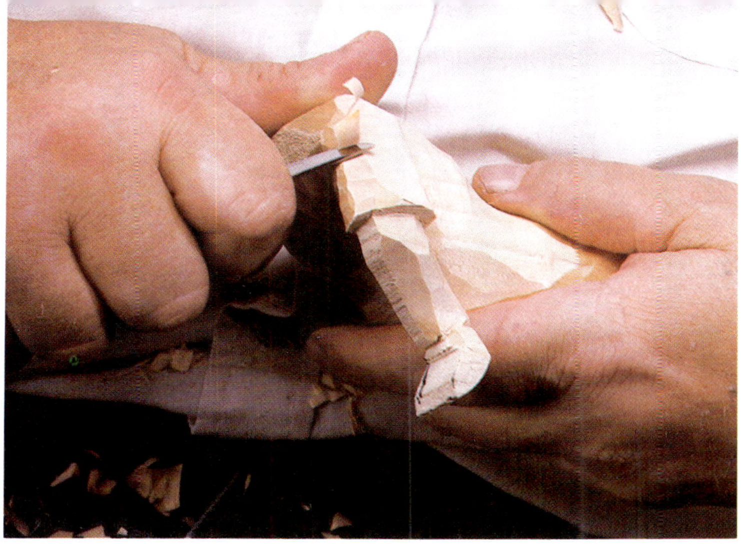

so we need to go back and thin the back.

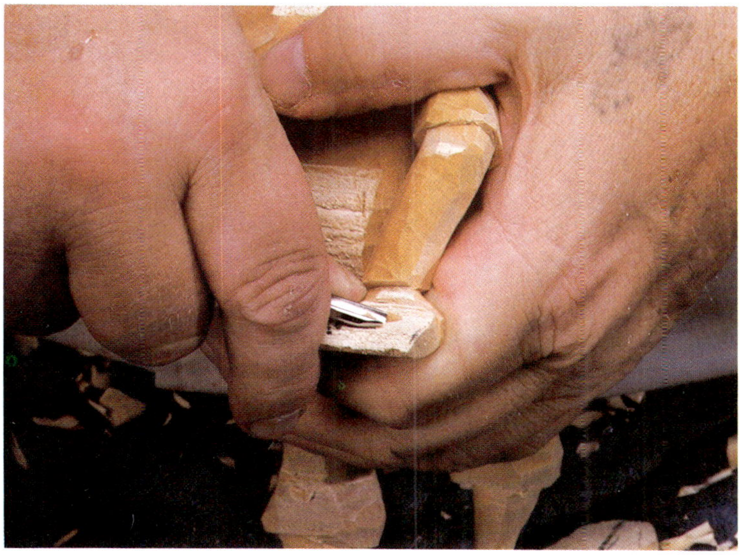

Use the half round gouge to make a hole in the palm cf the back hand for the baseball.

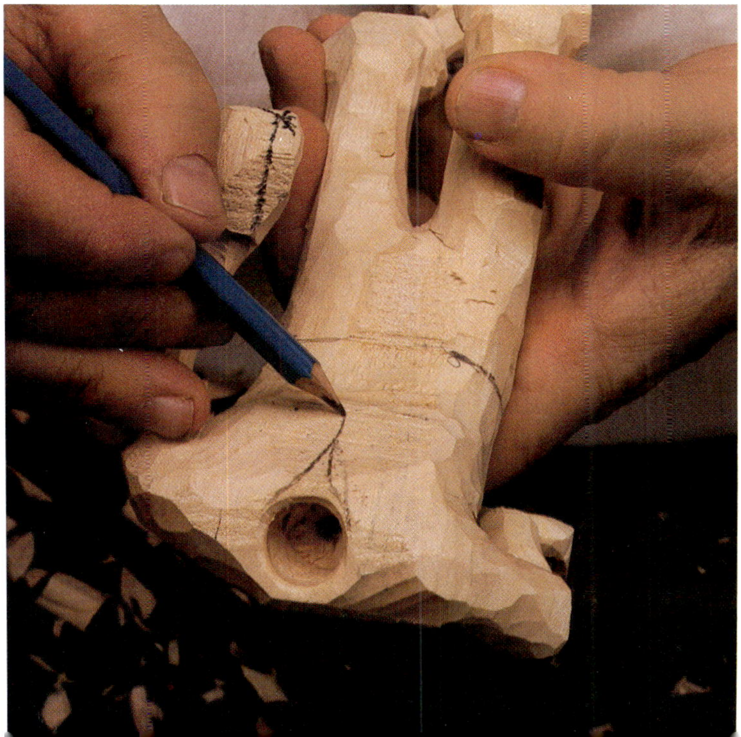

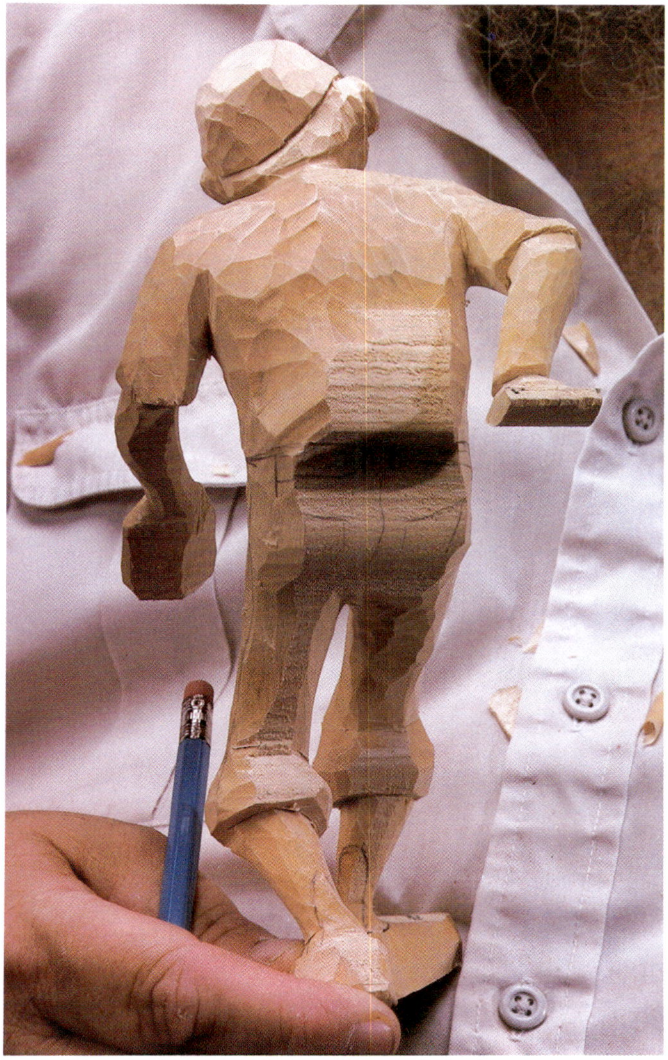

Draw in the uniform.

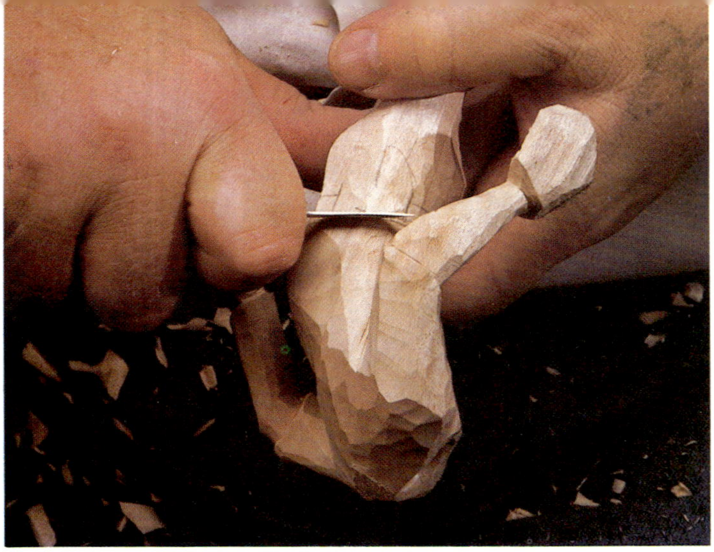

Cut a stop around the top of the belt.

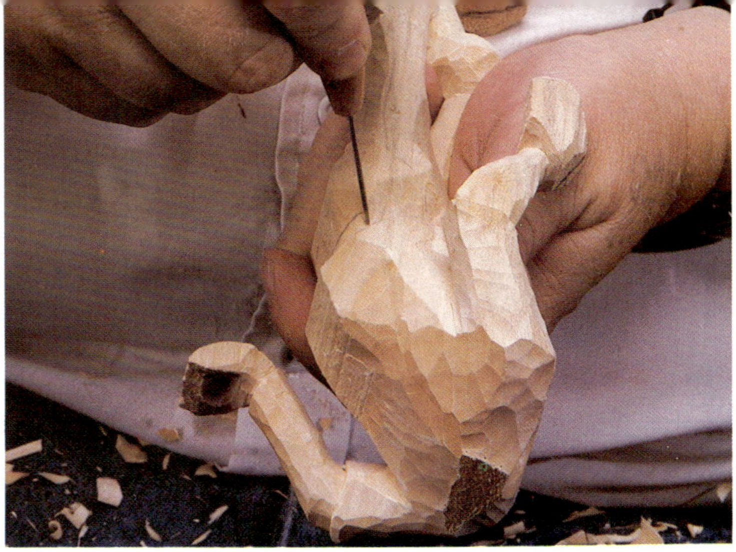

Cut a stop in the side of the belt loop...

Cut back to it from the pants.

and slice along beside it from the belt.

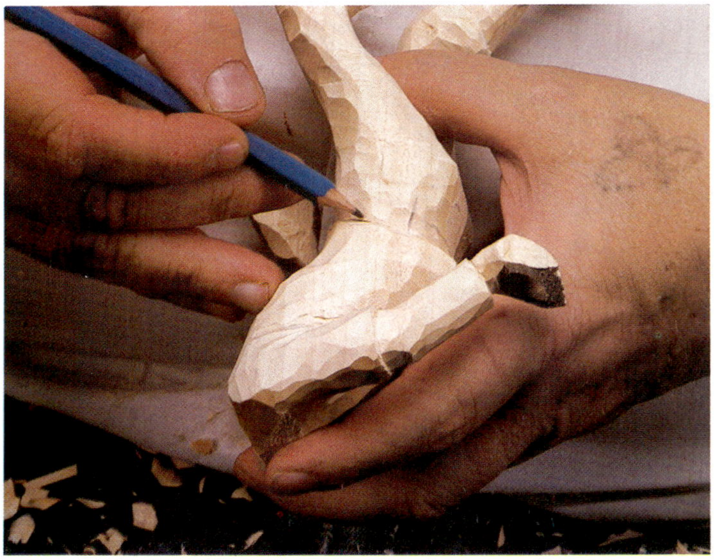

Since you cut away most of the marks for the belt you need to draw them back in.

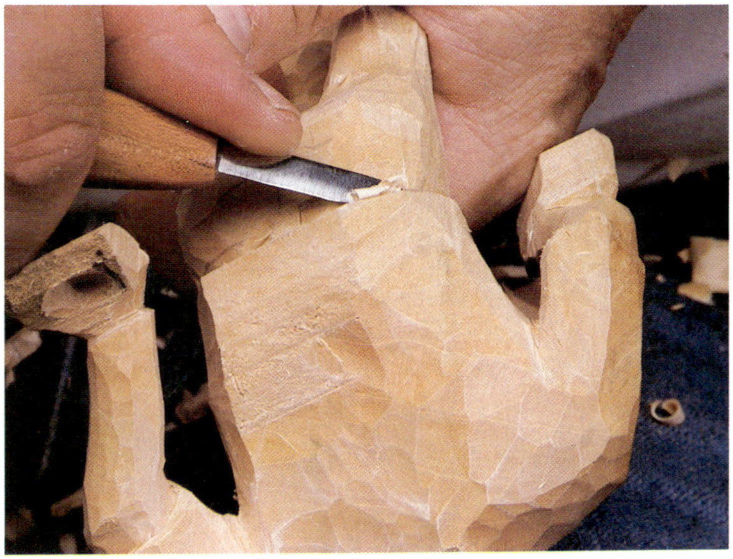

Clean and flatten the area between the loops so they look like they naturally go under the loop.

Draw in the bottom edge of the belt.

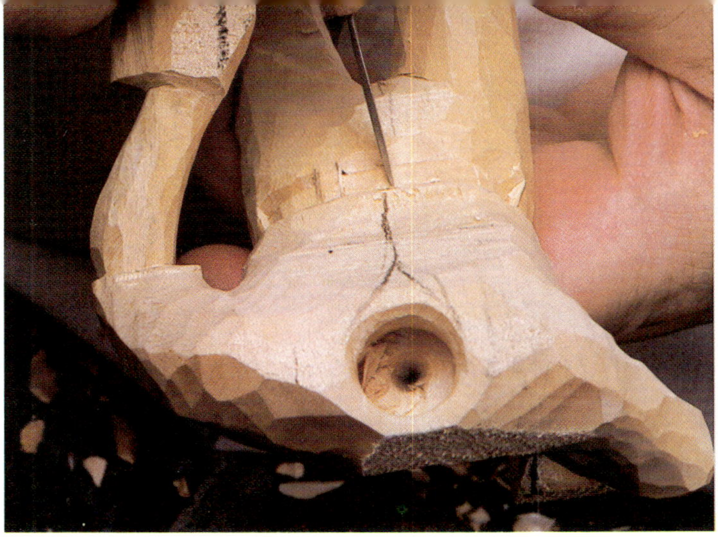

Cut into the belt to form the edge of the buckle.

Cut a stop in the bottom edge of the belt...

and trim back to it from the pants.

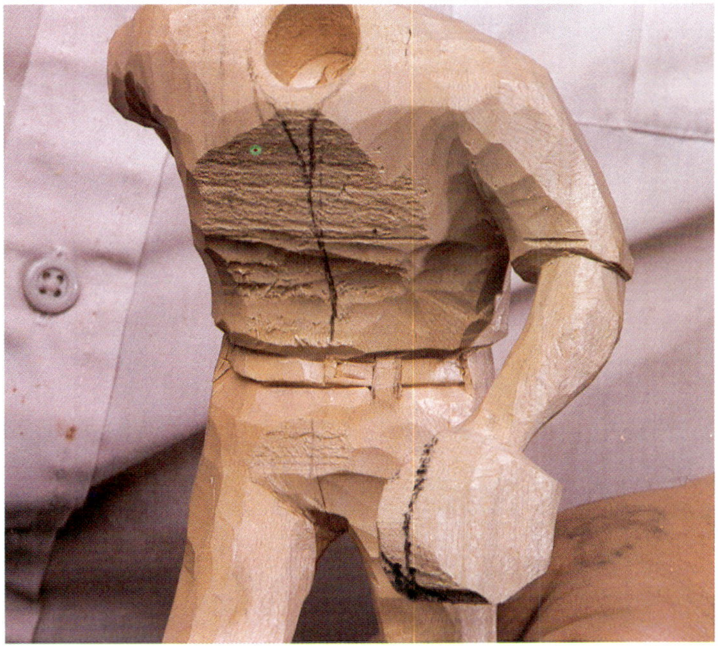

Clean out the inside a little to give it definition.

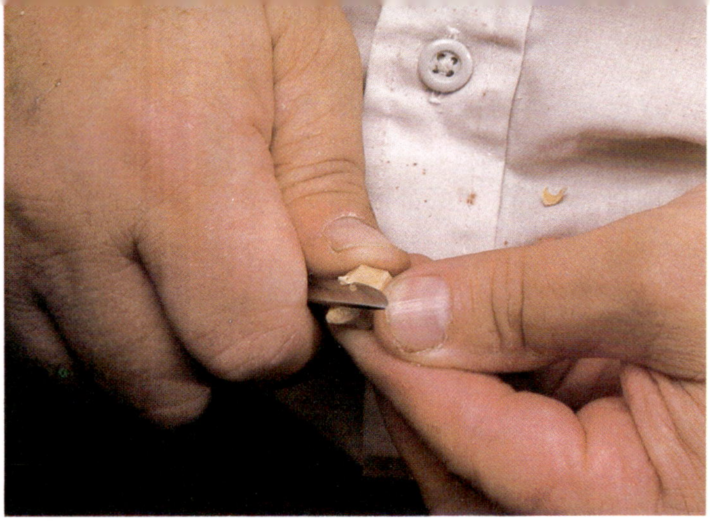

From a piece of scrap carve a baseball. Keep turning it so it stays nice and round.

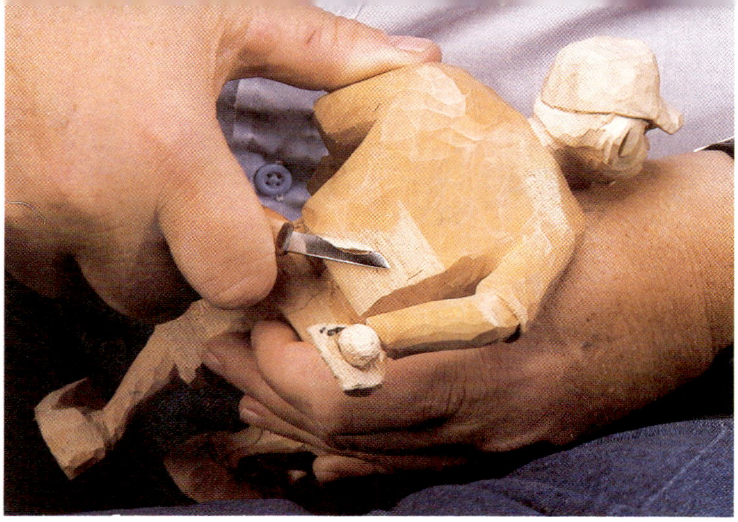

Go over the whole piece refining and smoothing as you go. Clean up any saw marks you may have left.

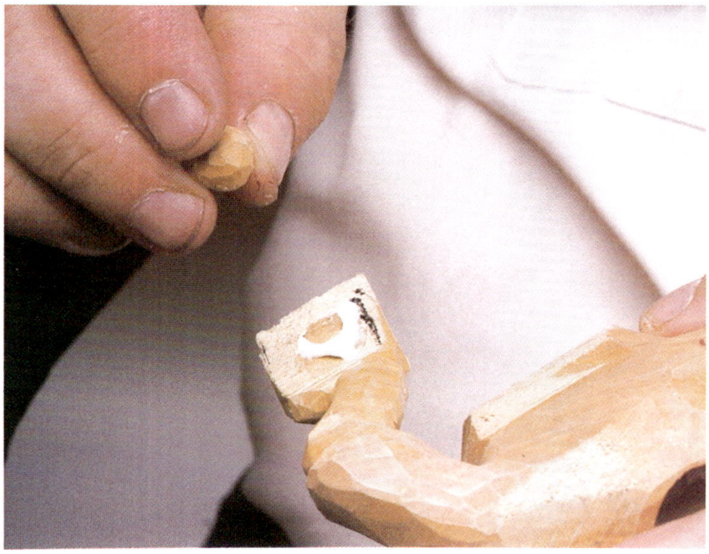

Apply a drop of glue to the hand...

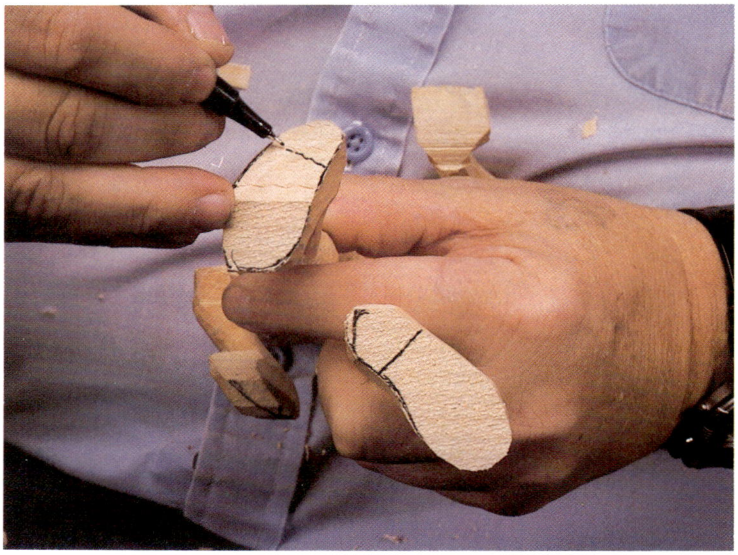

Mark the heels of the shoes.

and glue the ball in place.

Create the heel by cutting straight in at the corners...

and back to it from the sole. This creates the appearance of a heel, but leaves a flat surface for gluing.

The sole that is in the air needs to have the heel cut all the way across.

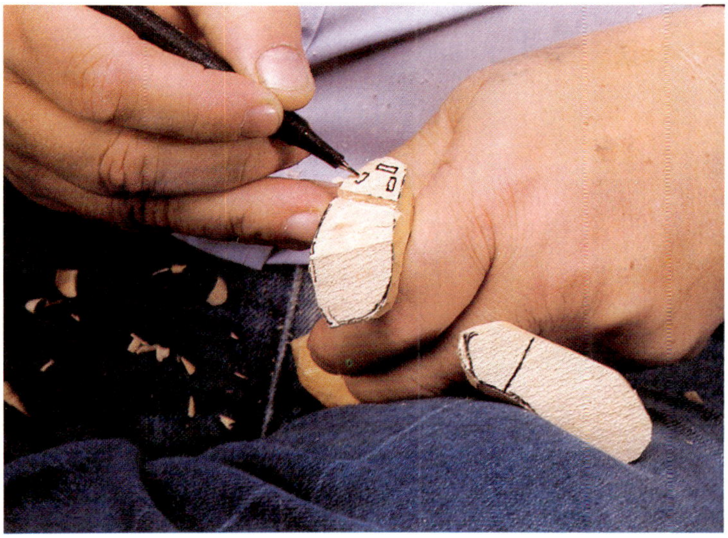

Also on this airborne heel, you will need cleats. Draw them in.

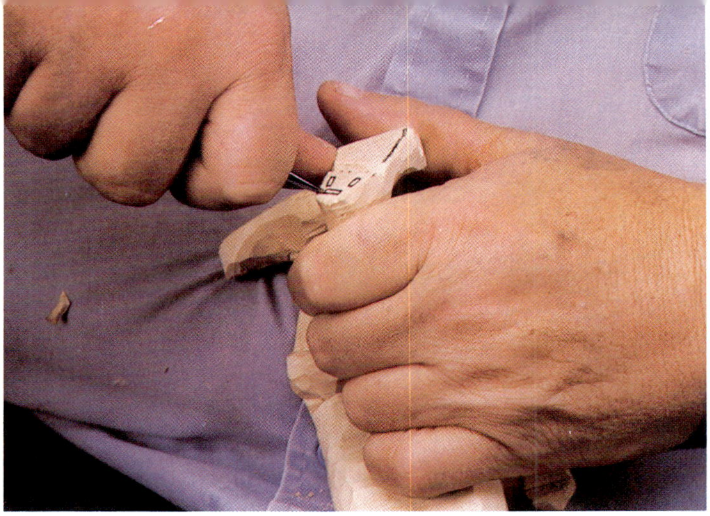

Score them lightly for a stop.

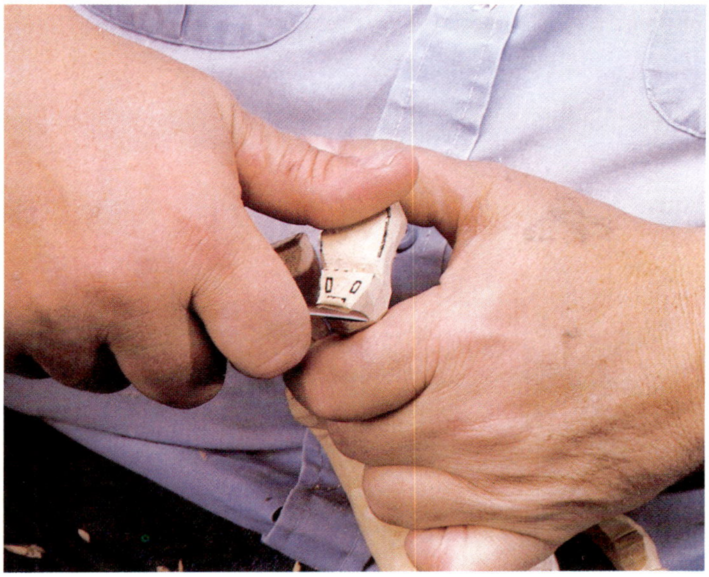

Cut back to the cleats from the heel. These don't need to protrude very much. All you need are just some lumps that represent the cleats.

The finished cleats. It is little details like this that make the carving better.

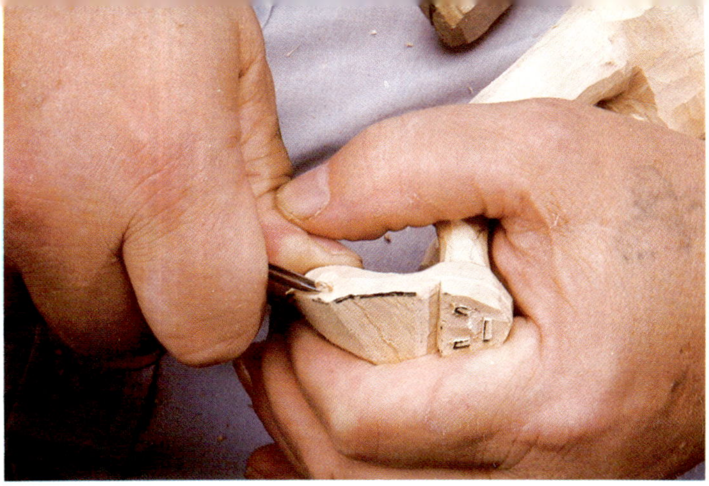

Create the line where the upper meets the sole with a good sharp gouge. If your gouge is not sharp enough, you can cut a stop around the sole, and cut back to it from the upper.

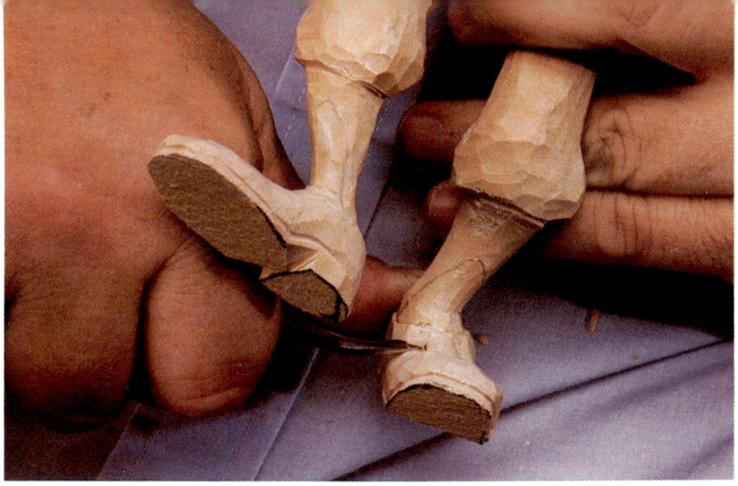

Shave along the line from the outside.

Round the toe of the shoe.

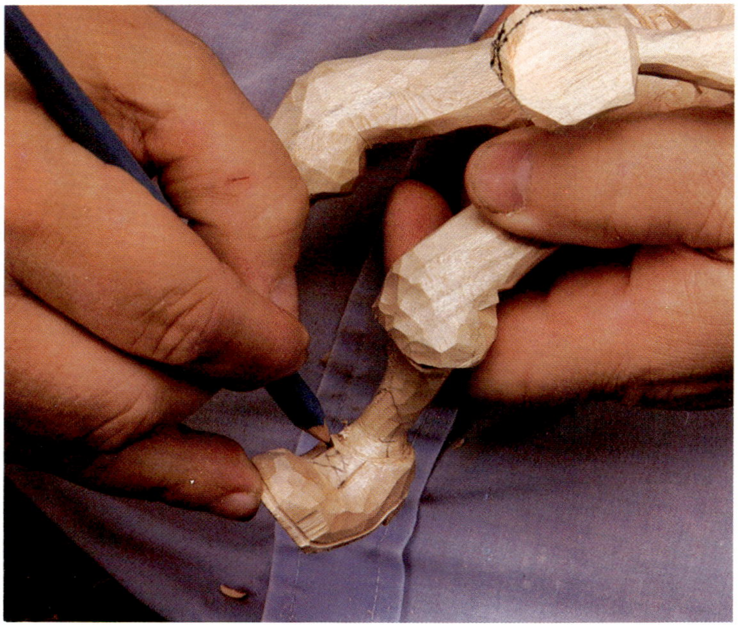

Laces are hard to do, and I usually try to hide them if I can, but on the baseball player, this is next to impossible. Draw in the lace lines.

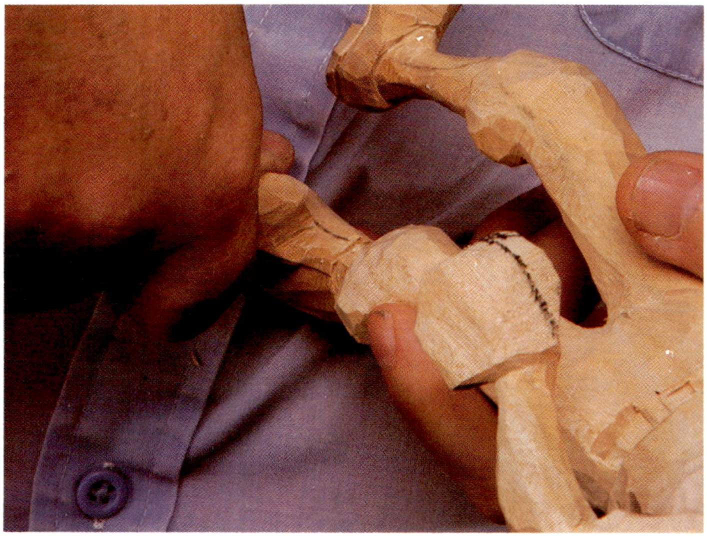

Draw the lines of the opening of the shoe. Cut a stop in the line.

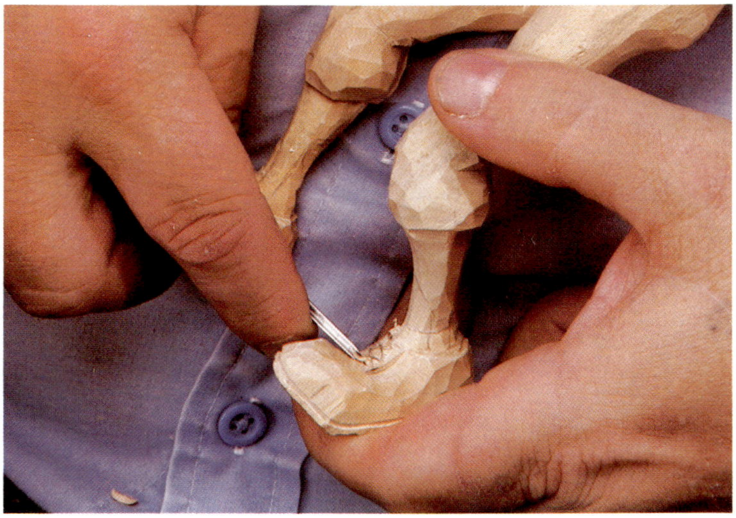

With a veiner go beside the lace lines, first on one side...

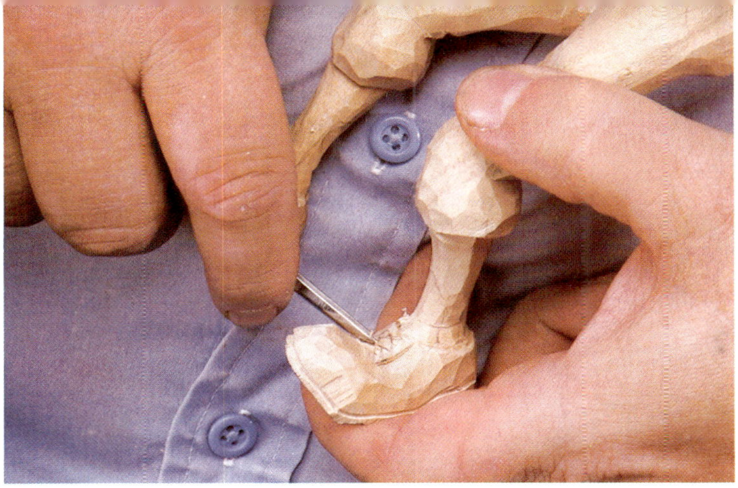

then on the other.

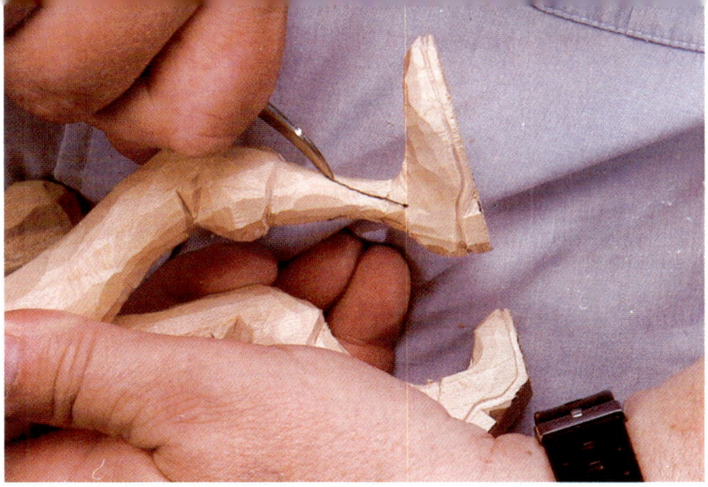

Cut a stop along the lines...

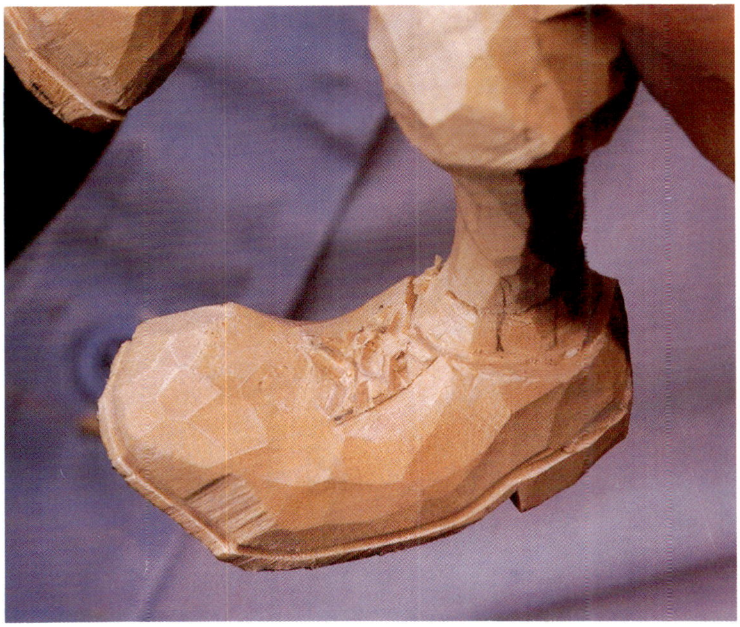

The result is a passable set of shoe laces.

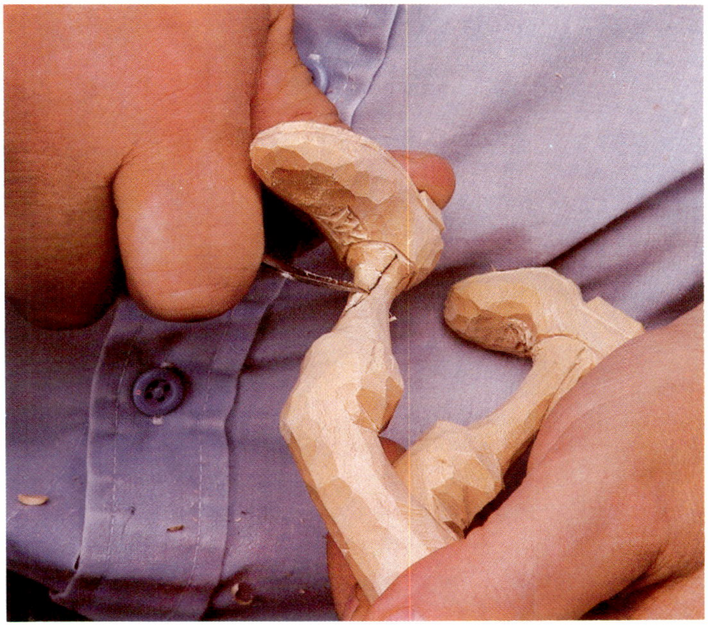

And trim back to it from the sock.

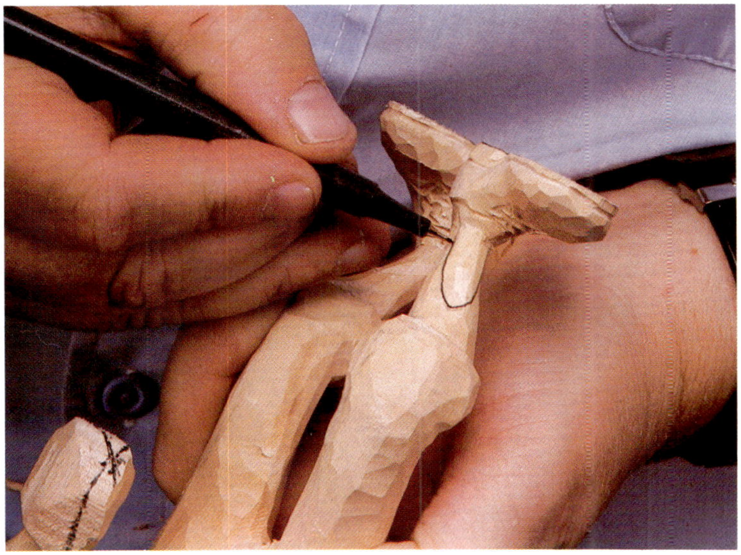

Draw in the colored "stirrups" for the socks.

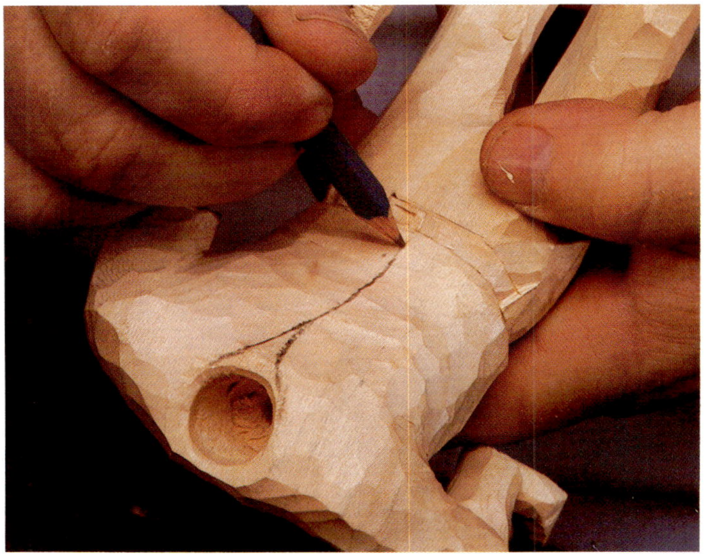

Remark the jersey.

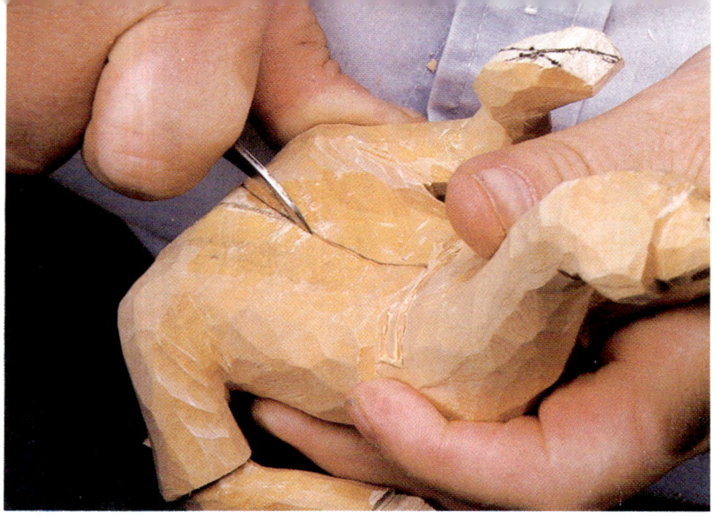

Cut stops along the lines.

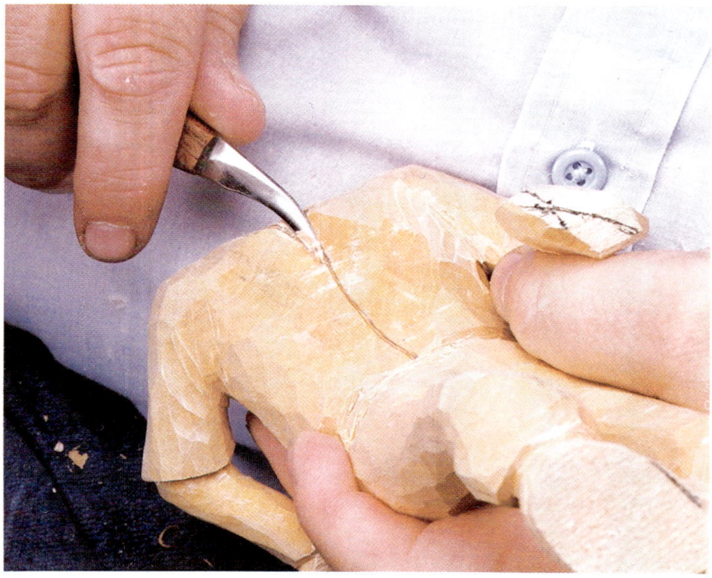

Clean out the "V" at the neck.

Cut back to the stop along the opening of the shirt.

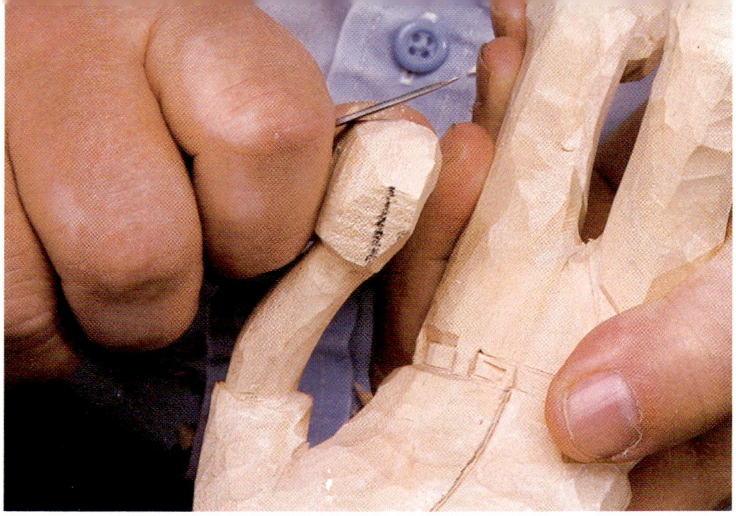

Carve the overall shape of the glove, removing old marks as you go.

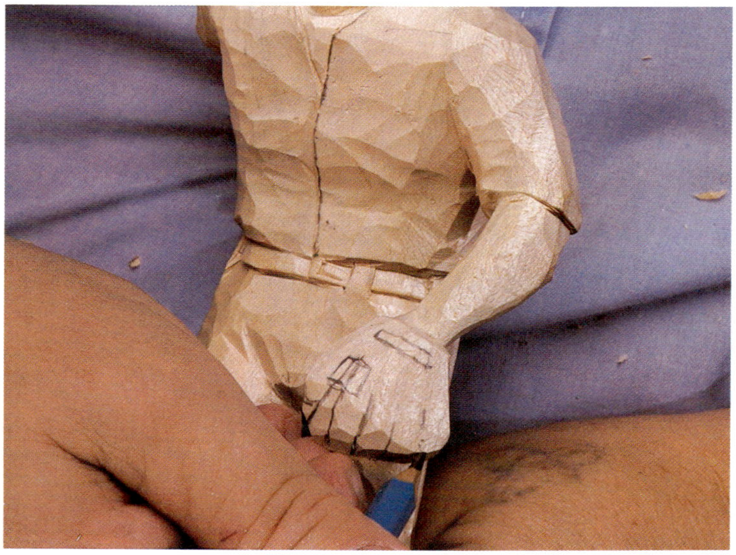

Draw in the details of the glove.

Use a U-shaped veiner to separate the fingers of the glove.

Cut a stop around the webbing of the glove...

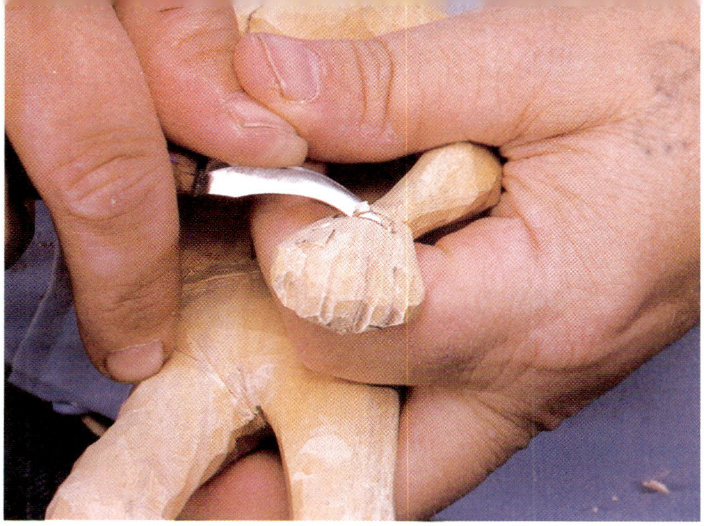

and chip it out.

and cut back to it.

Cut a stop at the end of the sleeve of the undershirt.

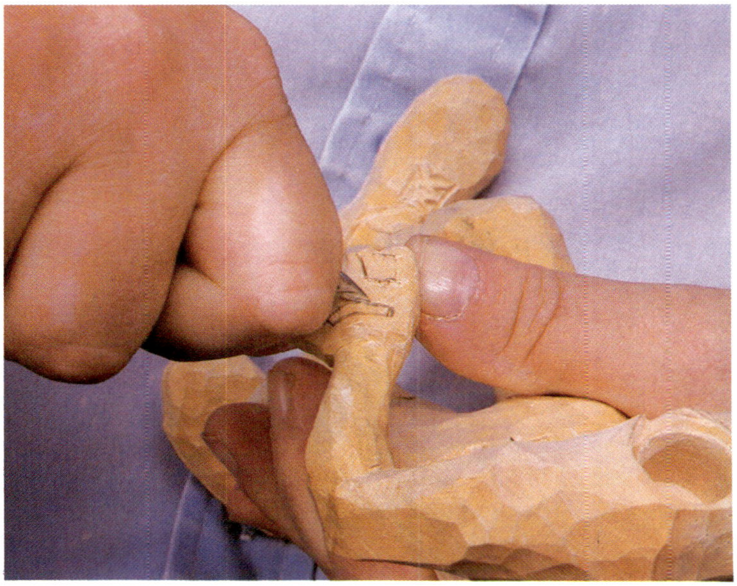

Cut stops around the opening in the back of the glove...

Come back to it from the wrist.

Use a gouge to clean out the palm of the glove. Notice the way my free thumb is used to support the glove and apply counter-pressure against the gouge. Without this counter-pressure the glove is likely to break.

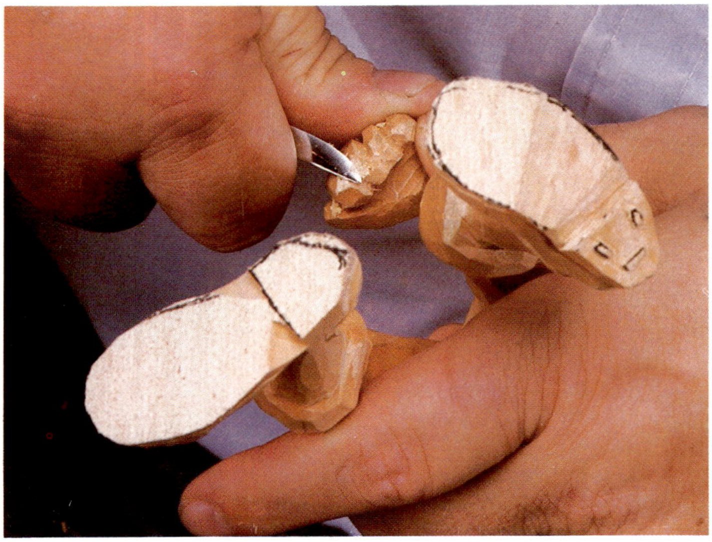

Clean up the glove with the knife.

Mark the thumb and the area to be removed on the ball hand.

Cut a stop on the inside of the thumb.

Trim back to the stop to remove the excess material.

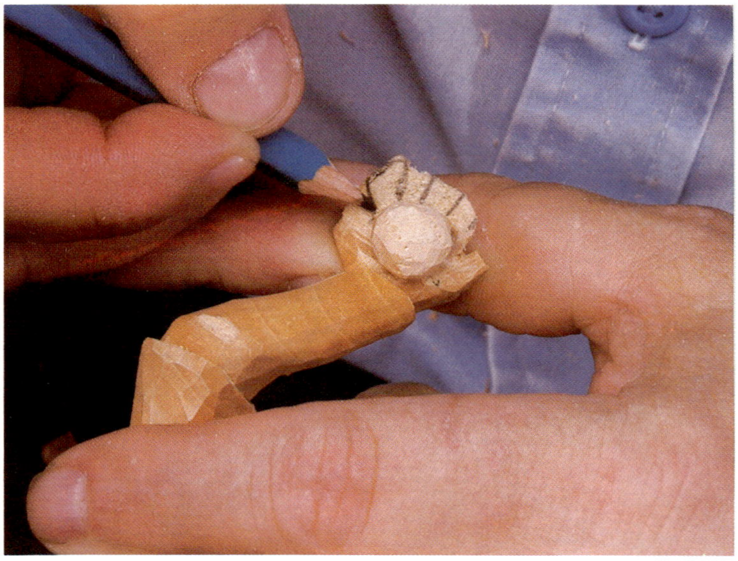

Draw the knuckles of the ball hand.

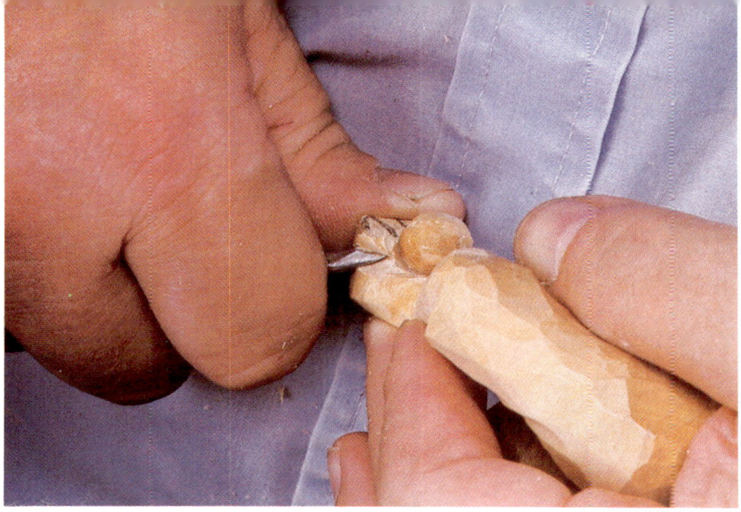

Trim the outside of the hand.

Take a slice between each knuckle.

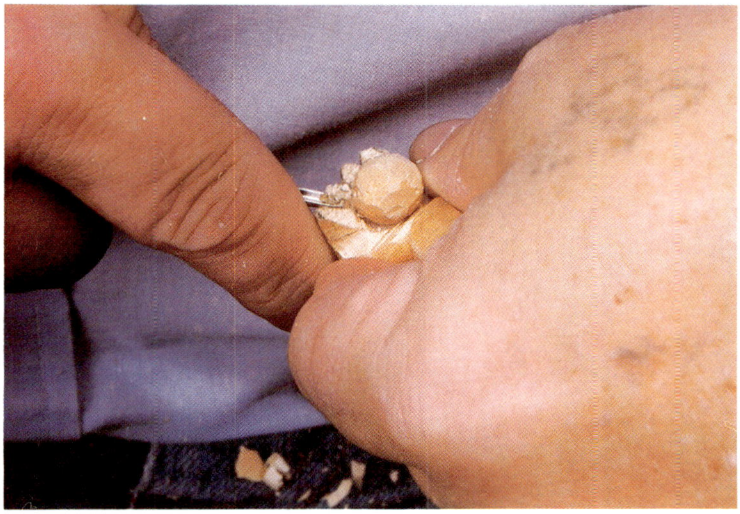

Use a veiner to separate the fingers. Be sure to hold the hand to give it support during carving. It is fragile and will break if not held properly.

Continue the separation lines on the back side of the hand.

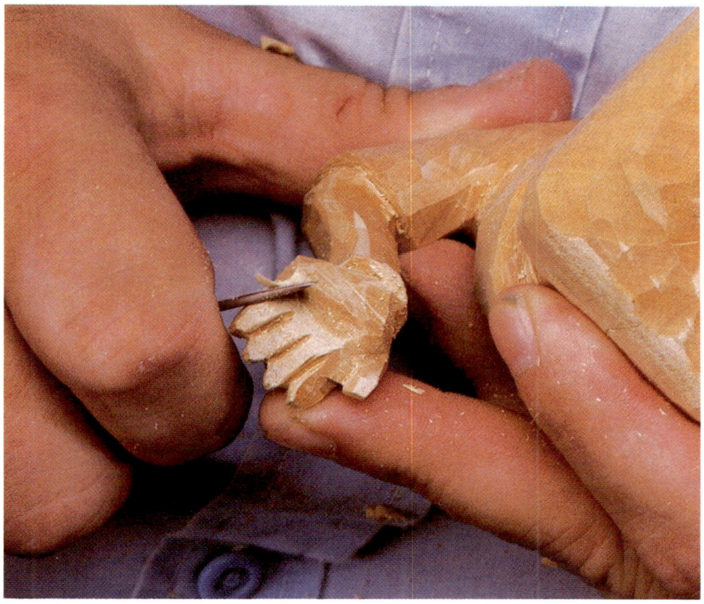

Trim the hand to size and round it off as you go.

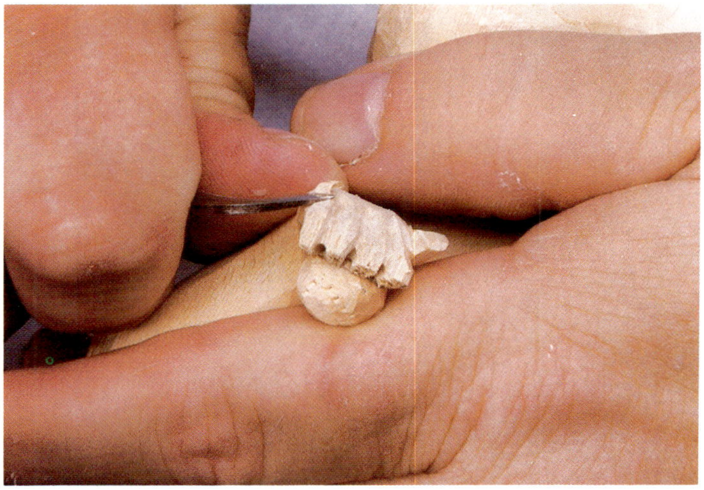

Continue to shape and size the hand until it looks right. This pitcher is holding the ball in a kind of modified knuckleball grip! For some people hands come naturally. For me they are just hard work.

Progress.

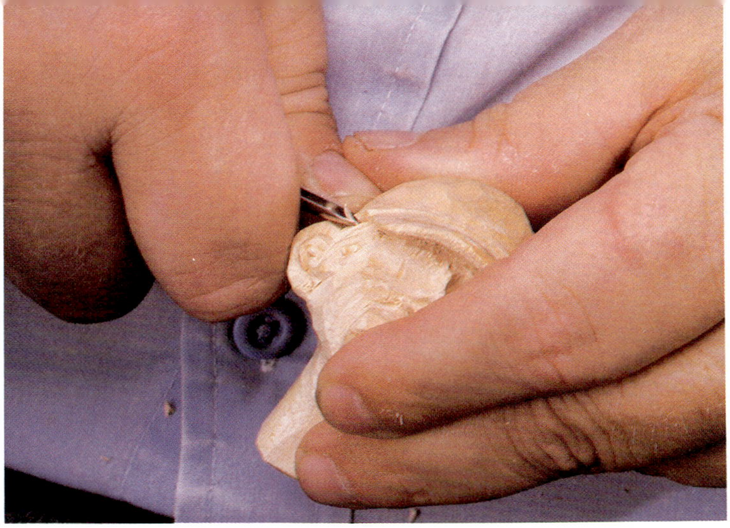

Create the hairlines using a small veiner.

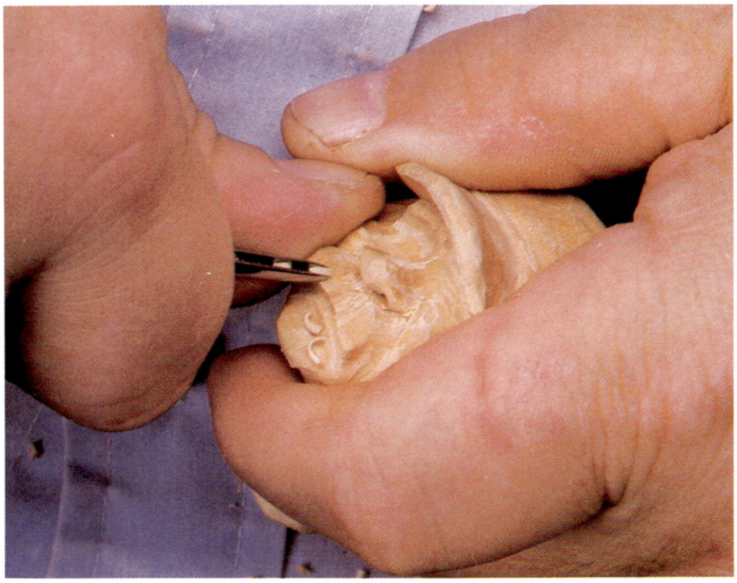

Continue to use the veiner in the moustache.

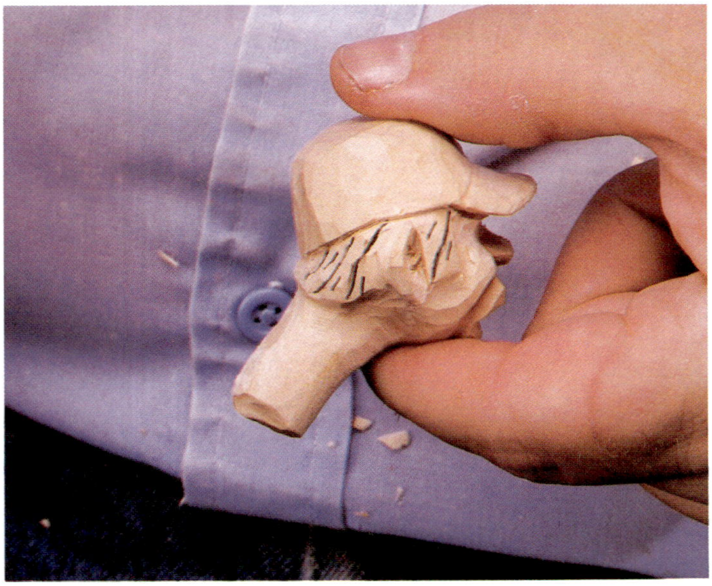

Return to the head and mark the flow of the hair.

Use the knife to clean up the face and soften the harsher lines.

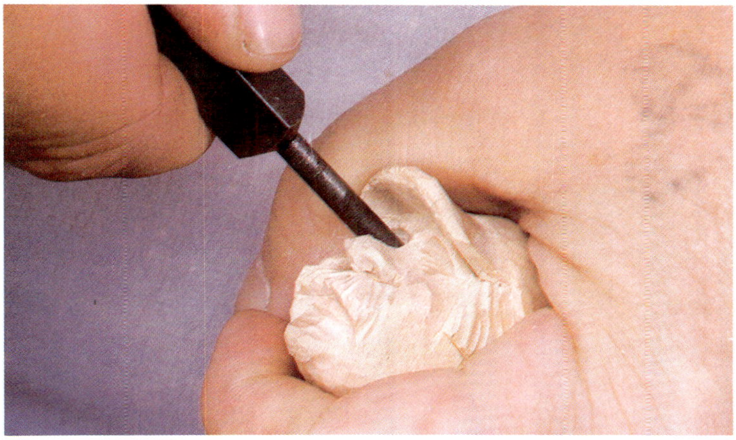

With a 5/32" eyepunch push and twist to form the left eye. By doing the left eye first, when you do the right eye it is just beside where you are working and your hand will not be in the way. This helps you align the eyes correctly. Of course, if you carve left-handed you should do it the opposite way.

Do the right eye.

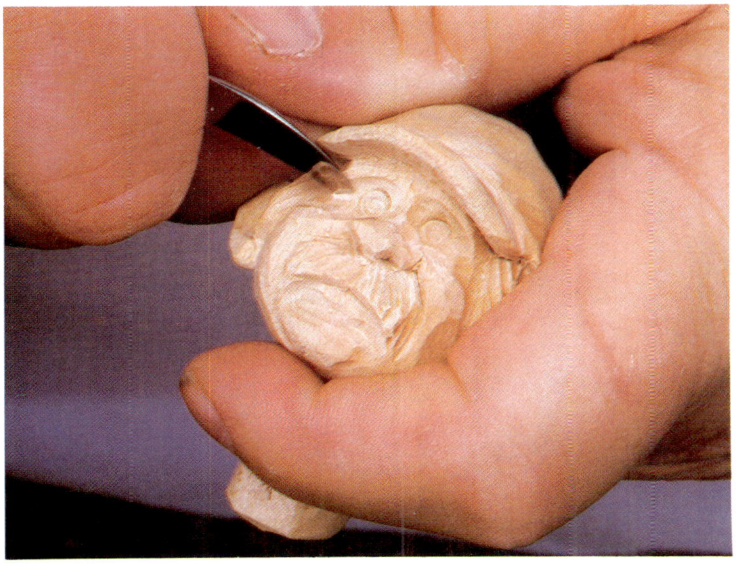

Create the outside triangle of the eye using three simple cuts. First, cut down along the line of the upper lid.

Second, cut along the contour of the eyeball into the corner.

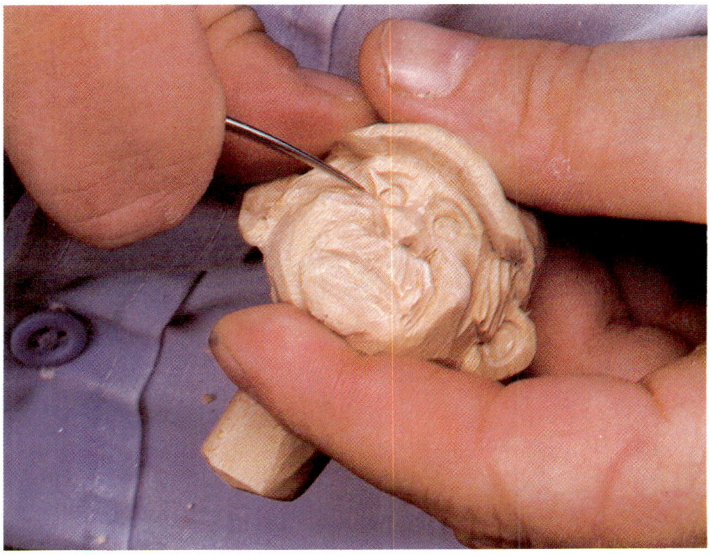

Third, cut up along the line of the lower lid. The triangle that define the outer corner of the eye should just pop out.

The same technique is used on the inside corner of the eye. Cut along the upper lid.

Then the lower lid.

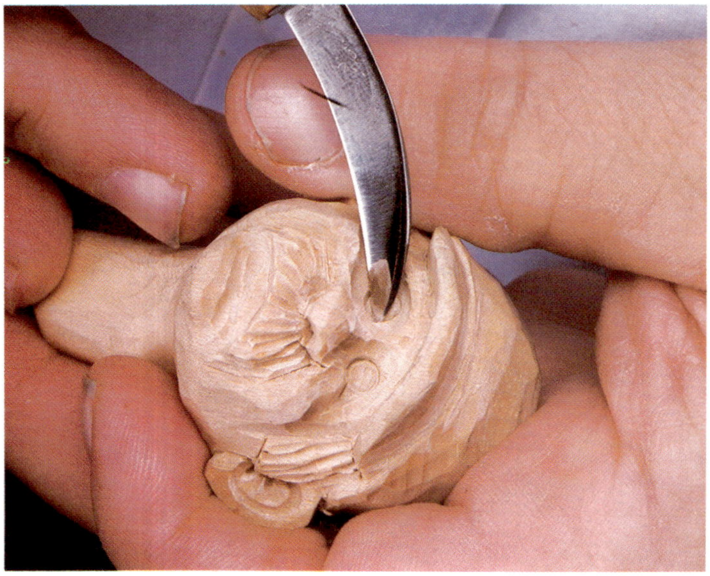

Then go along the contour of the eyeball to pop out the triangle.

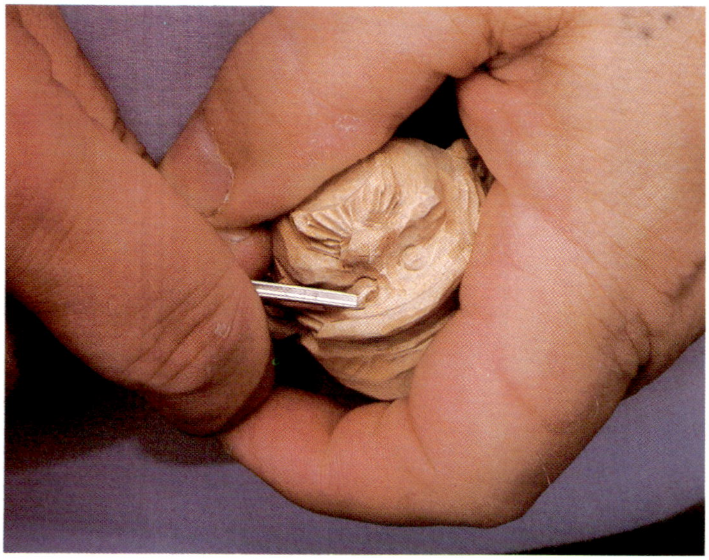

Use the veiner to create the upper eyelid.

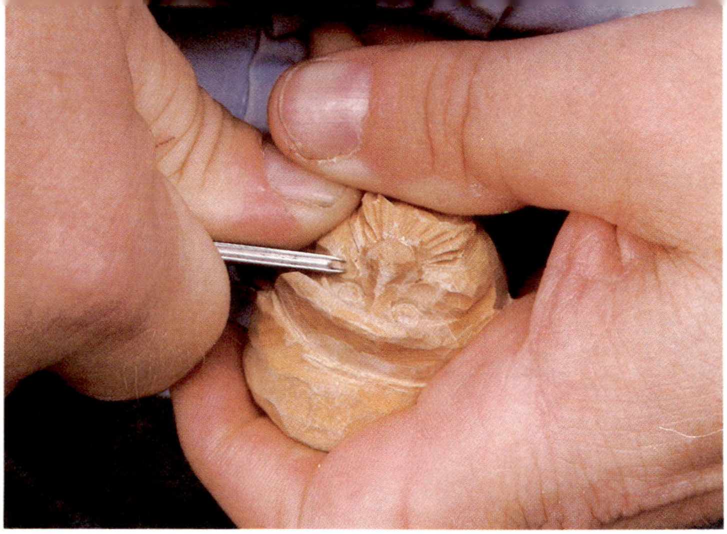

Use the same method to make a bag under the eye. This gives the figure a lot of character.

The head is complete.

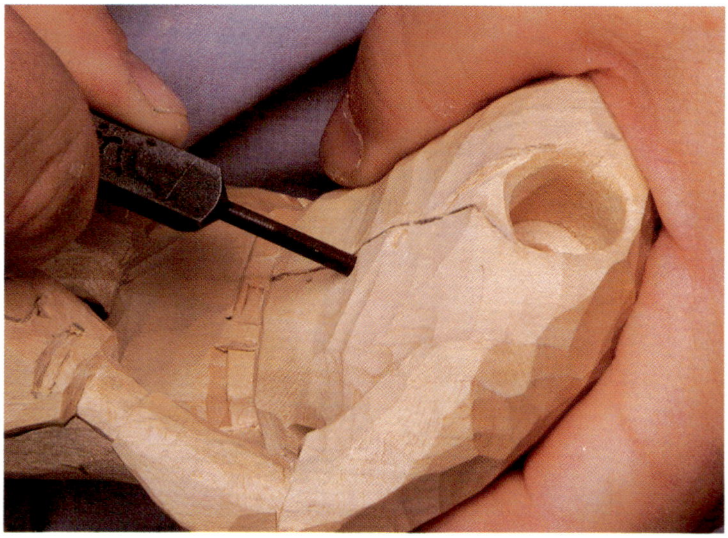

The buttons of the uniform are done in the same way as the iris of the eye. Use a small eyepunch and push and turn it. I do four buttons.

Use the veiner to score along the bottom of the belt loops to show that it is pieced in.

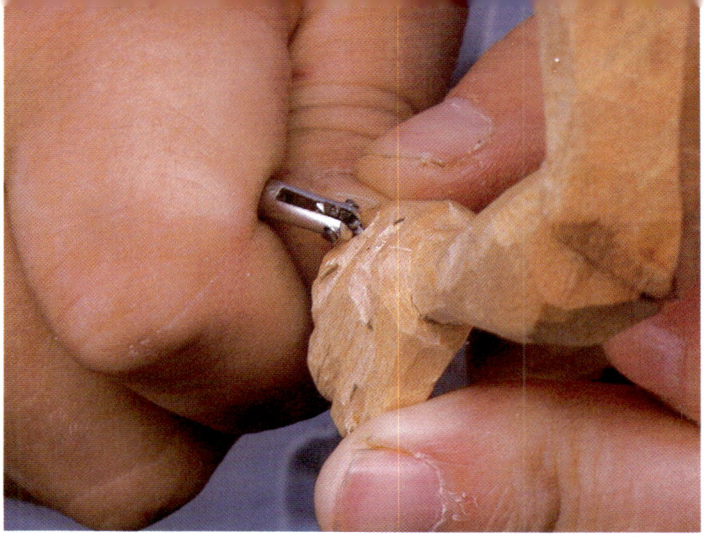

Don't forget the stitches on the glove and ball.

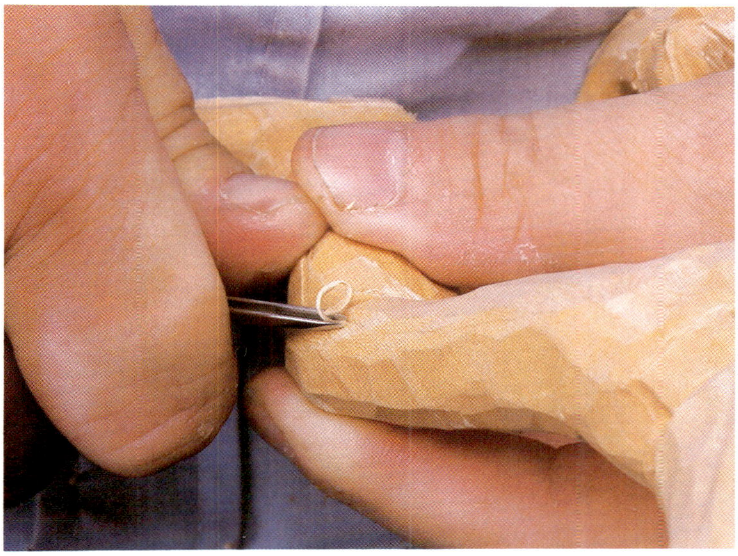

Use the same veiner to make the seams of the uniform, along the side of the legs, pockets, around the sleeves, the fly, and the crotch.

I use a Flair™ to draw the patches and pinstripes. It has good strong color and does not run when I overpaint it with my turpentine based paints. Whatever pen you use should be tested with your paints for compatibility! After sketching them in pencil, I draw in the arm patch...

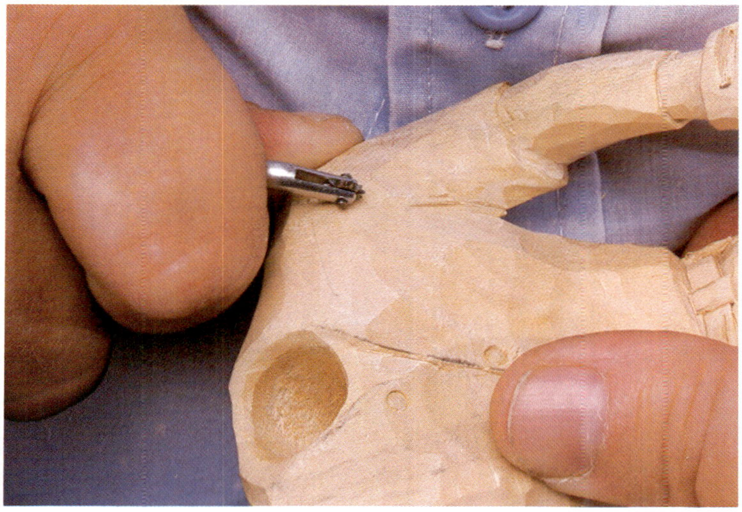

Go parallel to the lines of the seams with a fine tracing wheel.

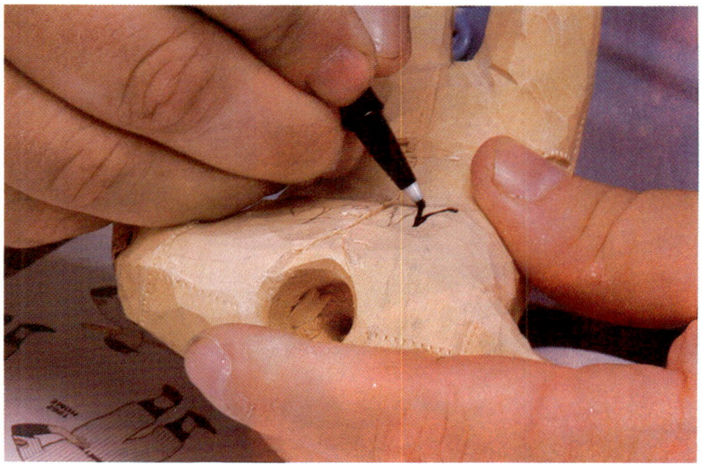

the chest decoration...

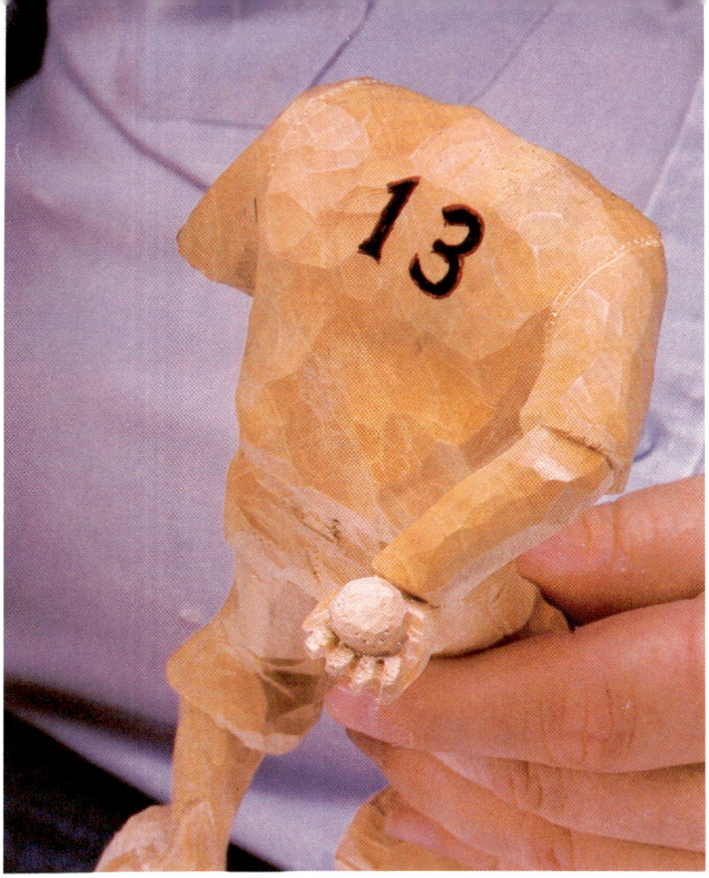

and the number on the back.

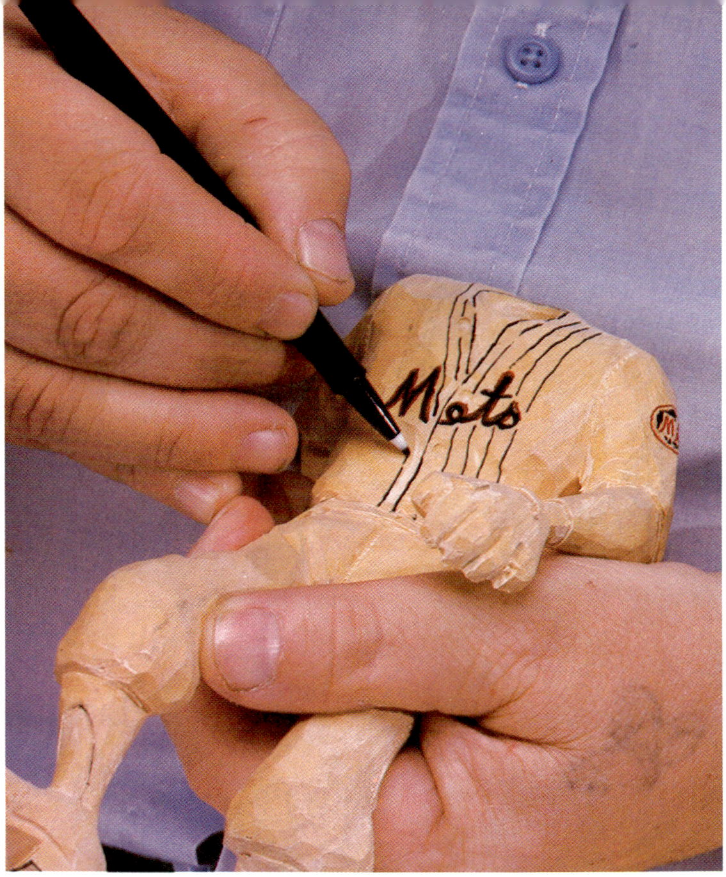

Work your way to either side from the middle, going from the belt to the shoulder seam.

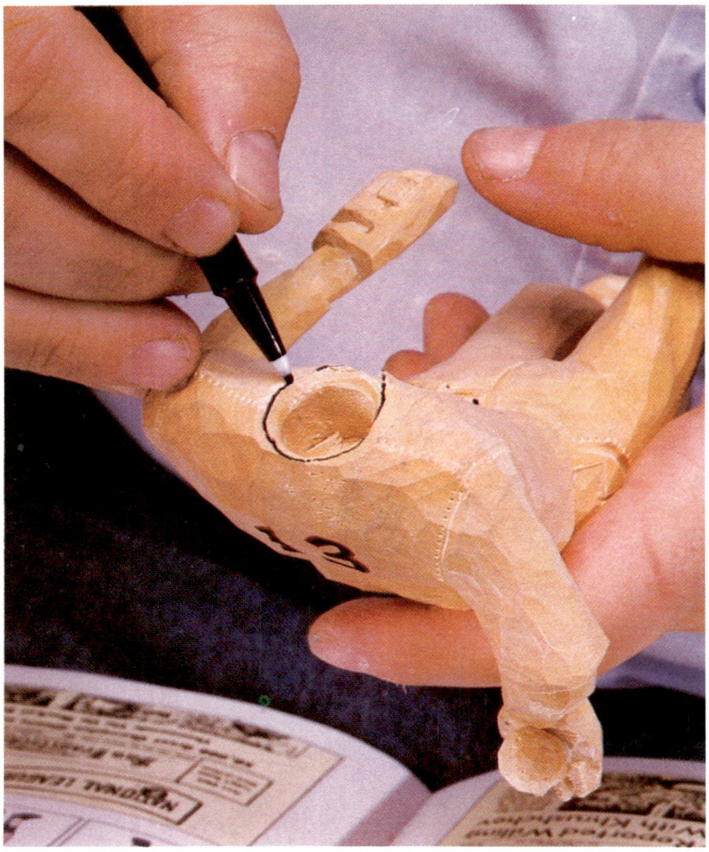

Start applying the stripes at the collar and opening of the shirt.

Again, start in the center of the back and work your way to either side. Try to make the lines meet at the shoulder seams, although that is not always possible.

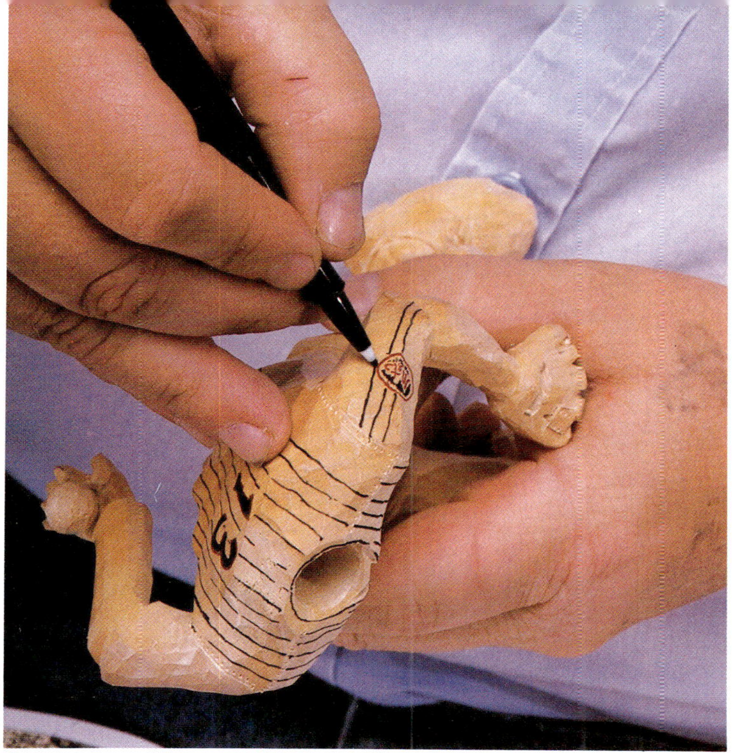

Continue in the same way on the sleeves.

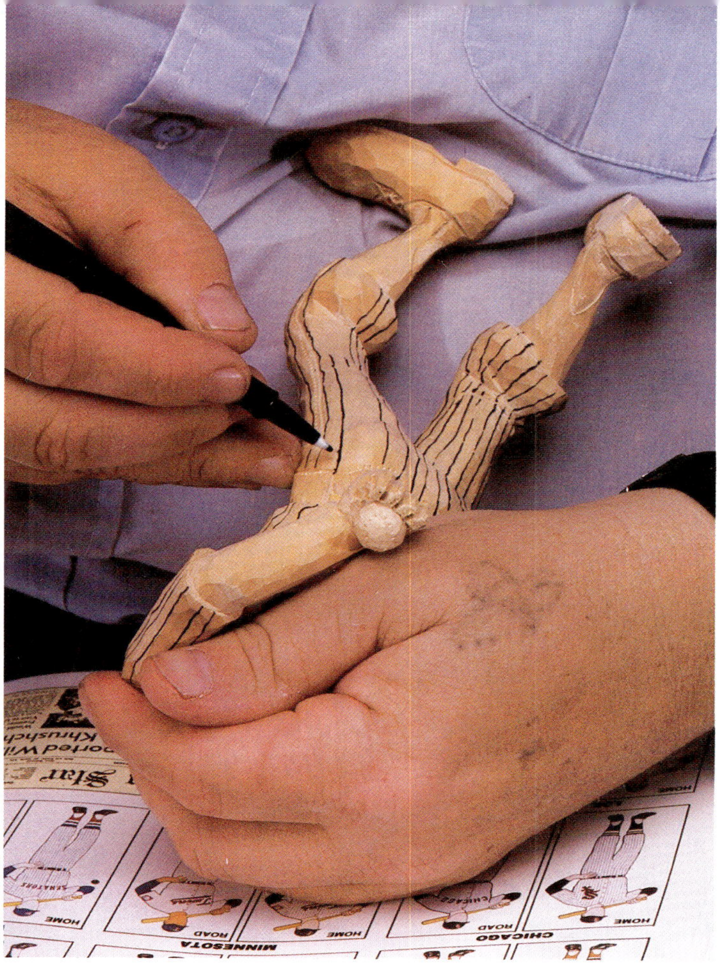

Fill in the pinstripes, working from the creases outward on each leg.

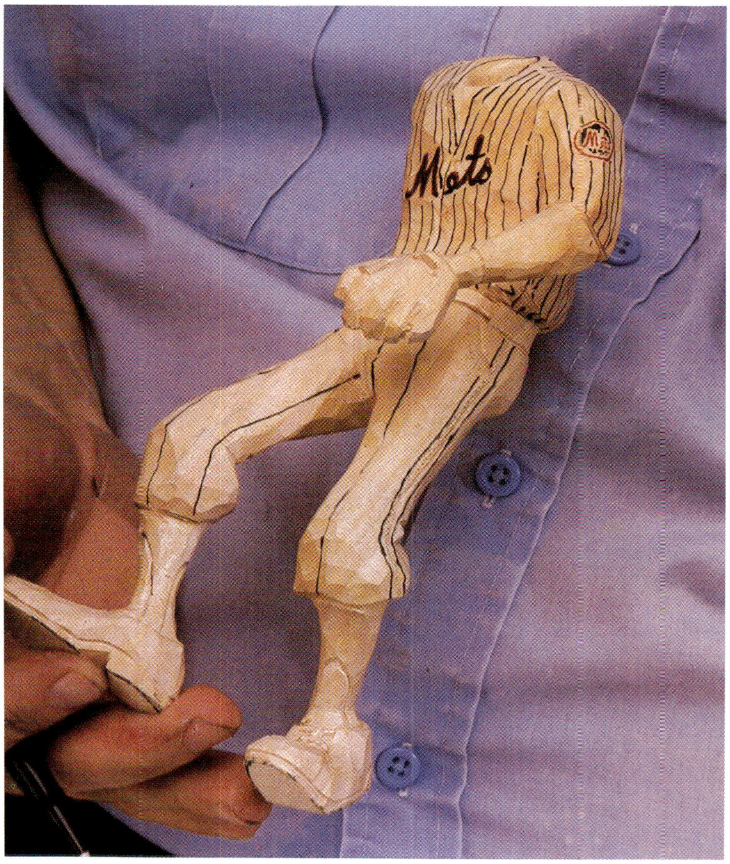

Start the pinstripes of the pants by setting the main lines. They are the fly, on either side of the outside seam, the inside seam, and creases in the back and front of each leg. These lines will basically divide the leg into four sections and help you avoid the problem of converging lines as you add pinstripes.

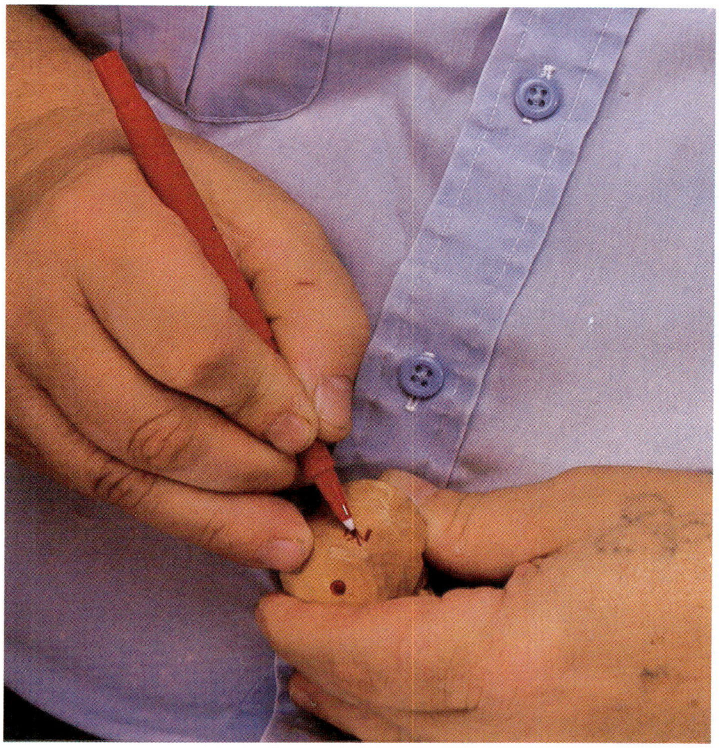

Use the Flair™ to color the button and the insignia on the cap.

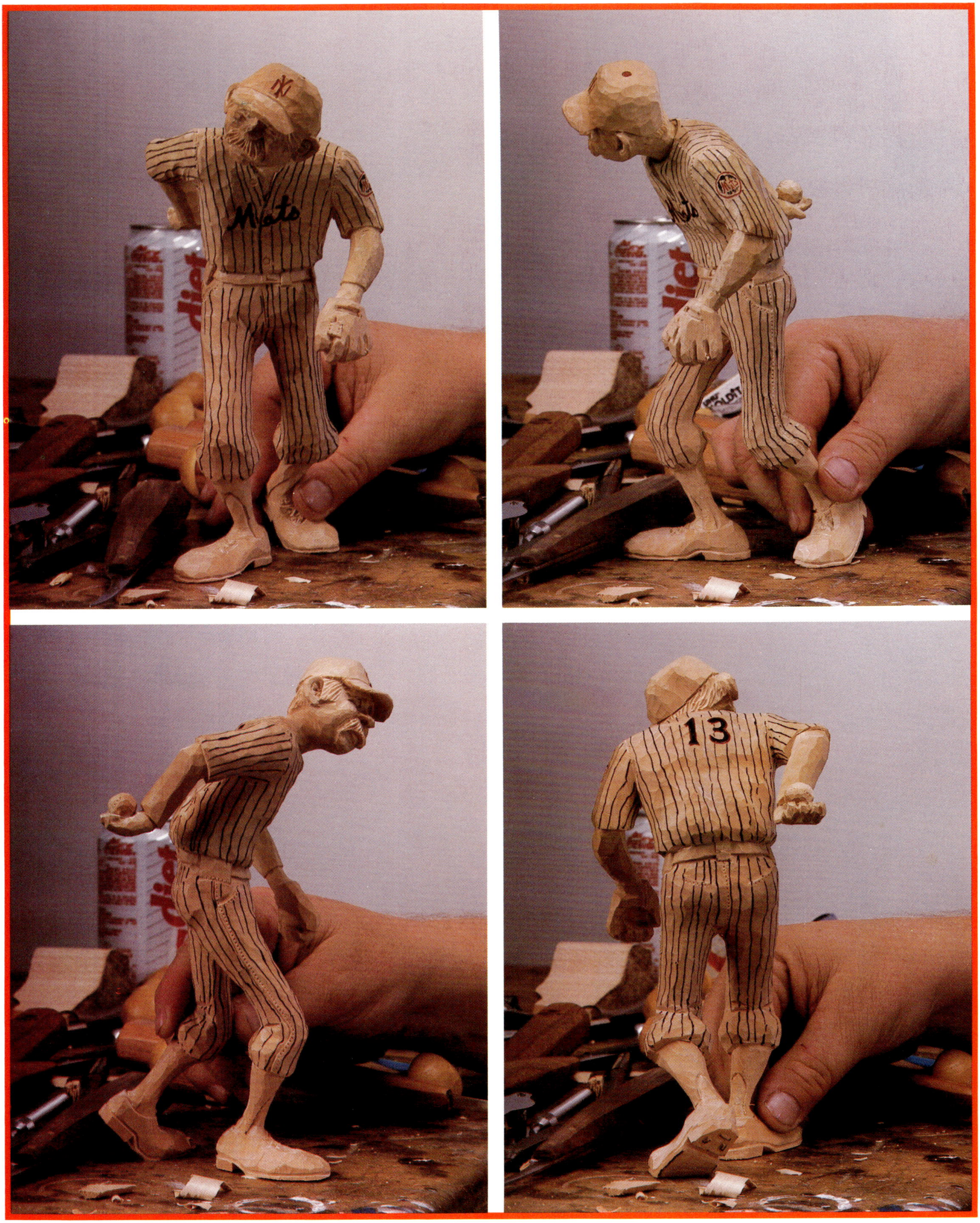

Ready for painting.

Painting the Pitcher

I use Winsor and Newton Alkyd tube paints for wood carving. These are thinned with pure turpentine to a consistency that is soaked into the carving, giving subtle colors. What I look for is a watery mixture, almost like a wash. In this way the turpentine will carry the pigment into the wood, giving the stained look I like. It has always been my theory that if you are going to cover the wood, why use wood in the first place. It should be noted that with white, the concentration of pigment should be a little stronger.

I mix my paints in glass juice bottles, putting in a bit of paint and adding turpentine. I don't use exact measurements. Instead I use trial and error, adding a bit of paint or a bit of turpentine until I get the thickness I want.

The juice bottles are handy for holding your paints. They are reclosable, easy to shake, and have the added advantage of leaving a concentrated amount of color on the inside of the lid and the sides of the bottle which can be used when more intense color is needed.

Apply flesh tones to the face. The color I use is a mixture of tube flesh with raw sienna and white. This makes it less pink and more realistic.

Add dots of red to the cheeks, the tip of the nose, the chin, and the lips, and blush it in with a dry brush.

You might also add a touch to the ears and the back of the neck.

Start applying the white paint to the uniform at the arm.

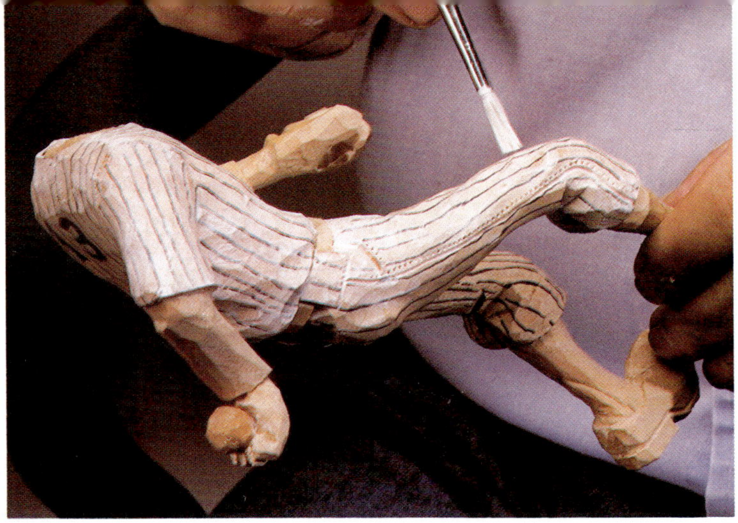

The pants are done in the same way.

Continue onto the jersey.

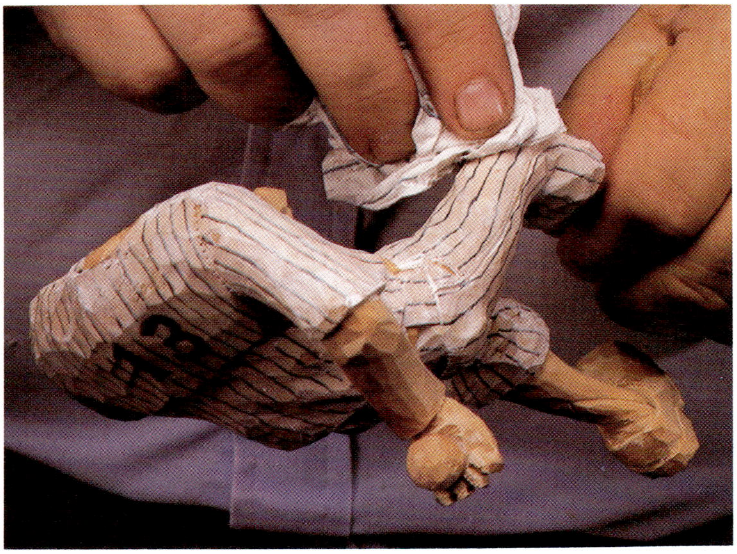

Blot away excess spots with a paper towel.

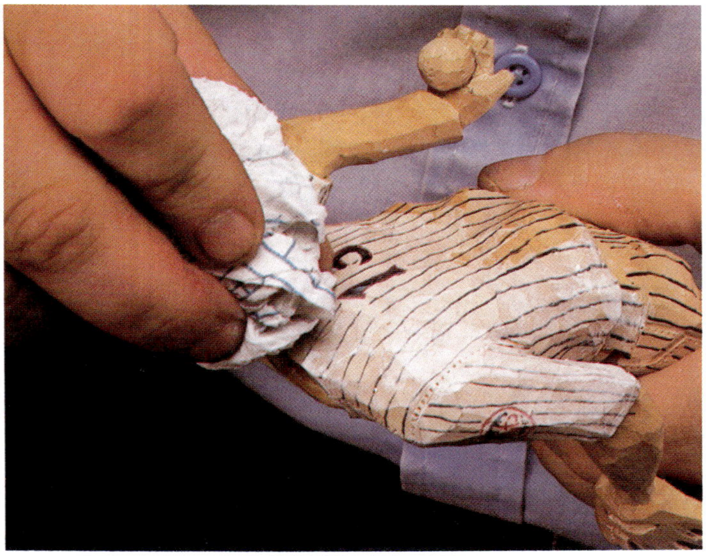

I paint over the insignias, and go back an wipe it off. You can paint around them if you like, but this softens them up a bit, which I like.

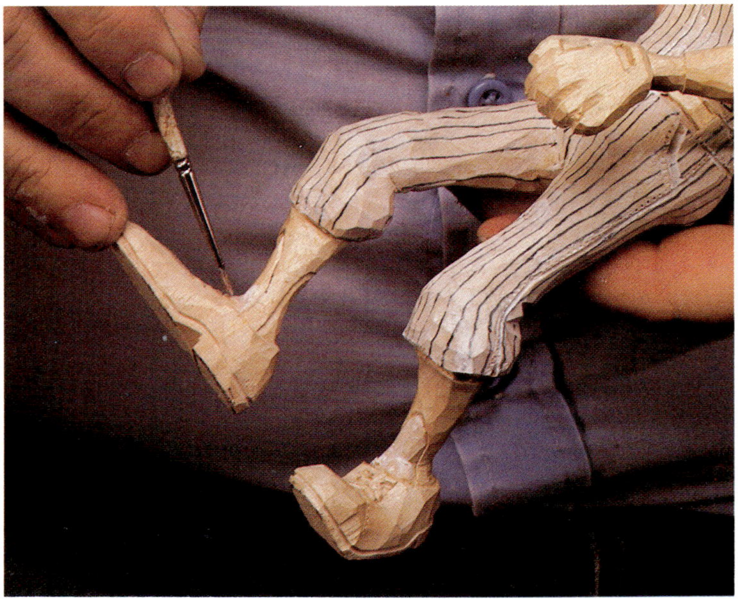

The last steps for the white are the socks, the ball...

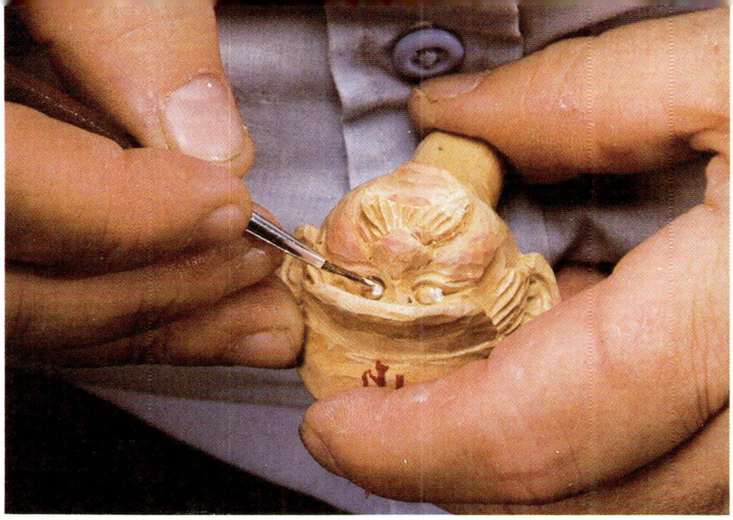

and the eyeball. For the eyeball use a very fine brush.

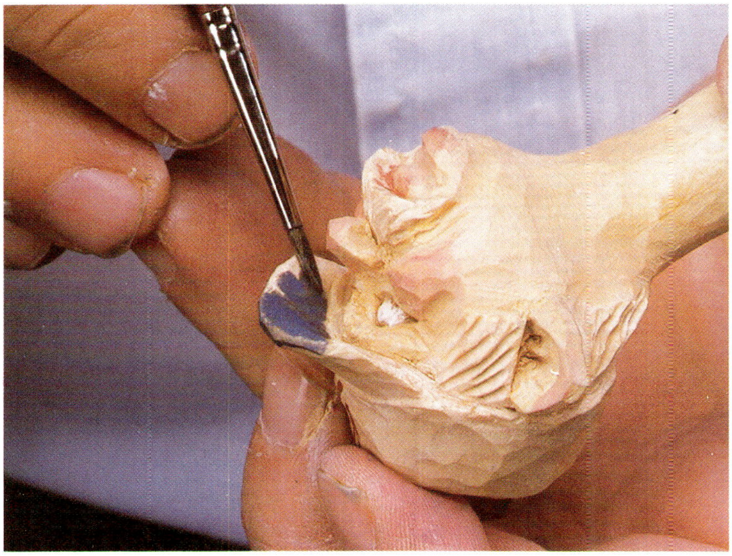

Switch to blue for the cap. Start with the underside of the bill to reduce the bleeding of the paint.

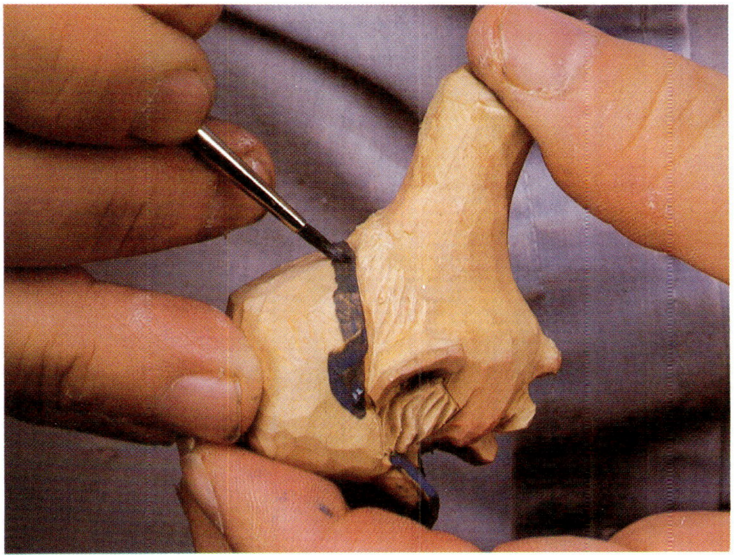

For the same reason, paint the bottom edge of the cap around the back and over the ears.

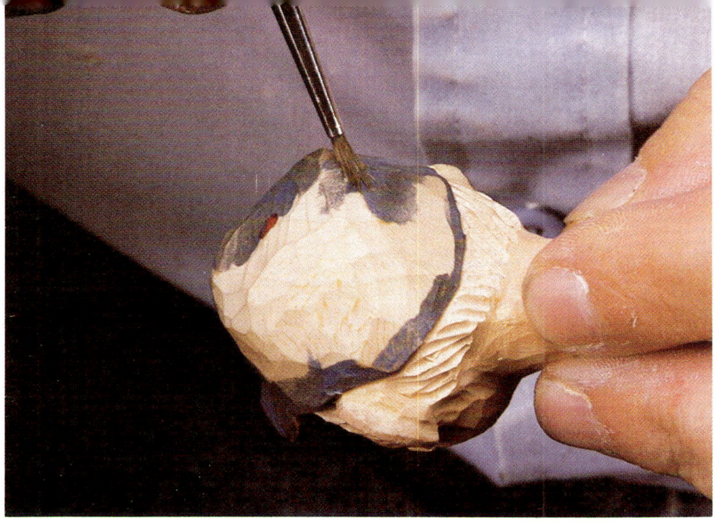

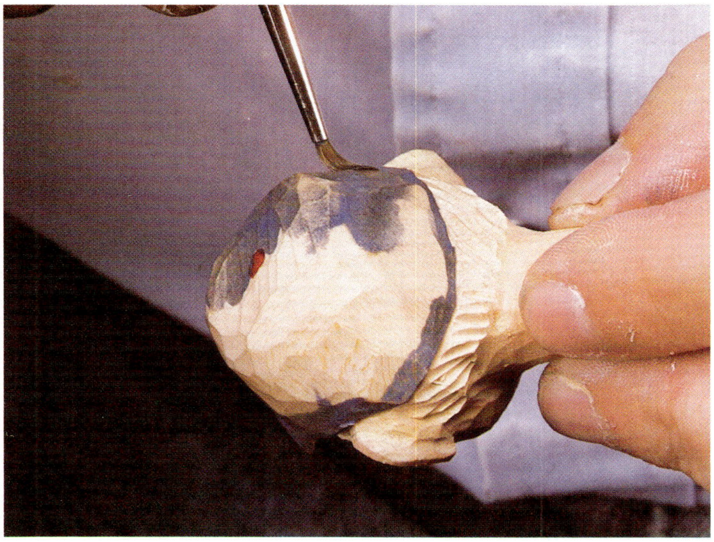

Paint the rest of the cap.

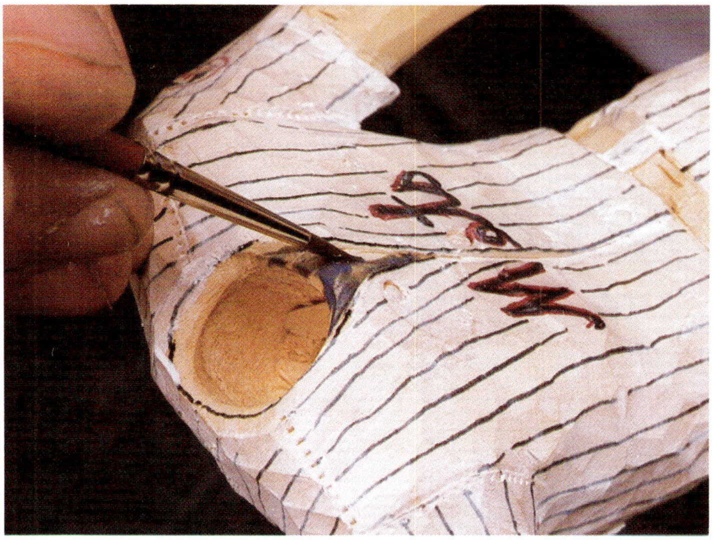

On the body paint the neck, sleeves, and "stirrups" of the socks blue.

Now I need to go back to the flesh tones for the hands and the little bit of the arm that shows. Truth be known, I should have done it earlier, but plumb forgot.

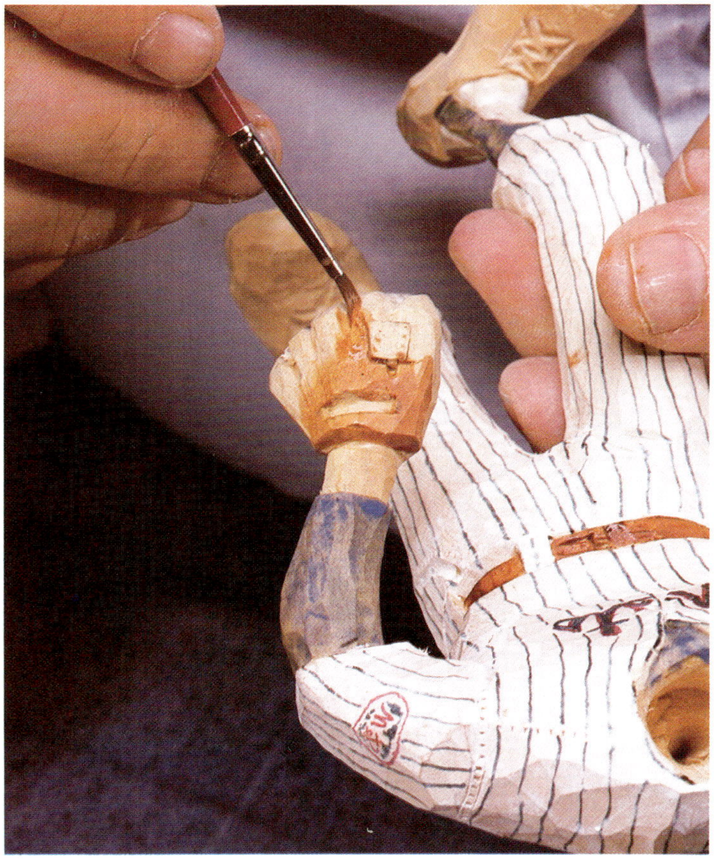

Burnt sienna is used for the glove and the belt.

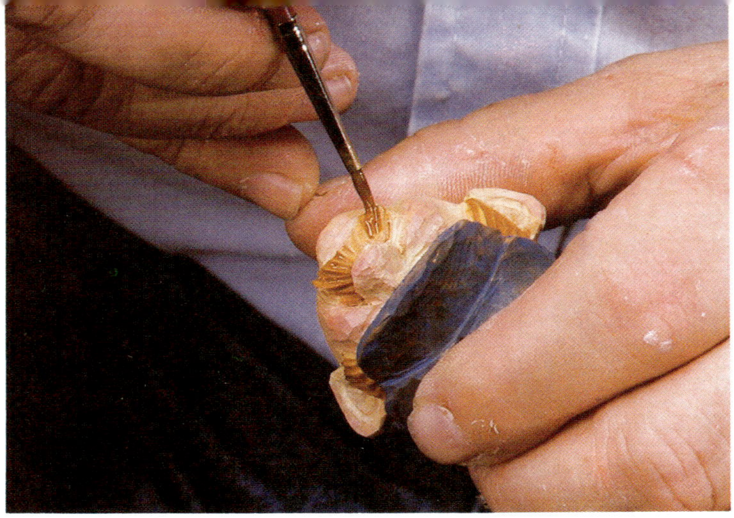

I've chosen to paint the hair with raw sienna, though other colors wouid work as well.

The iris will be painted with a mixture of blue and white. I use the lid for mixing.

Apply the paint to the iris so the figure looks straight on and a little up.

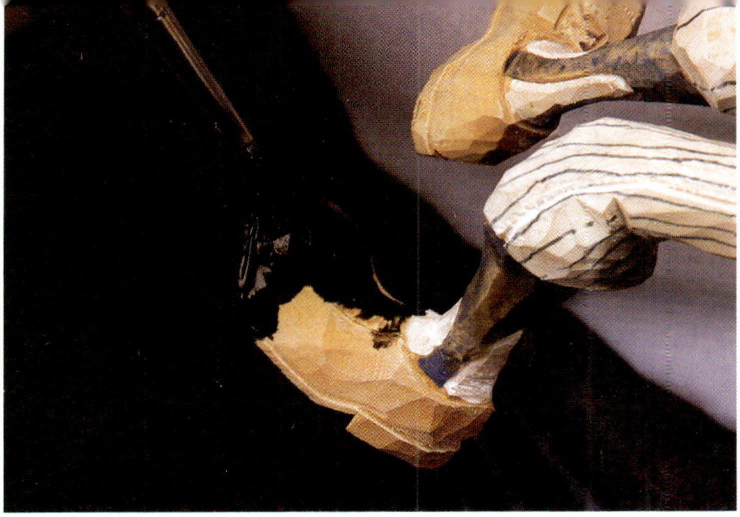

Paint the shoes black. Go over the cleats, even though they will later be painted with metallic silver.

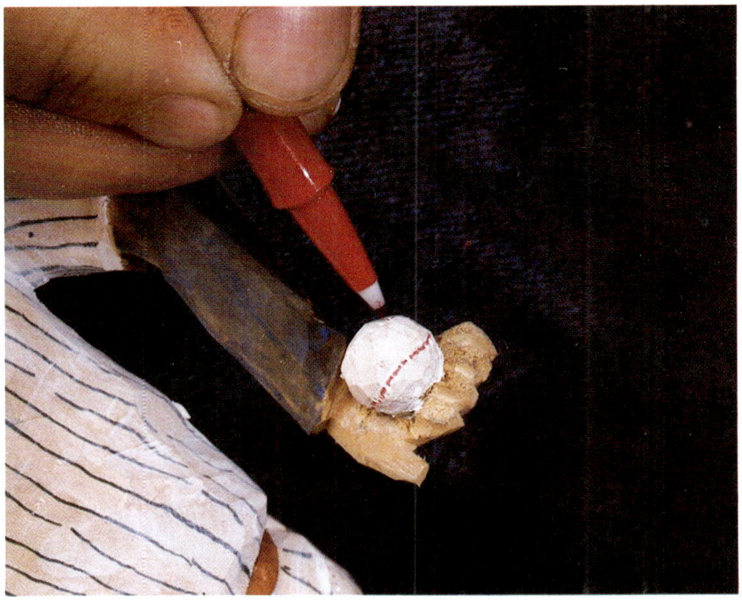

With the red Flair™ mark the stitches of the ball.

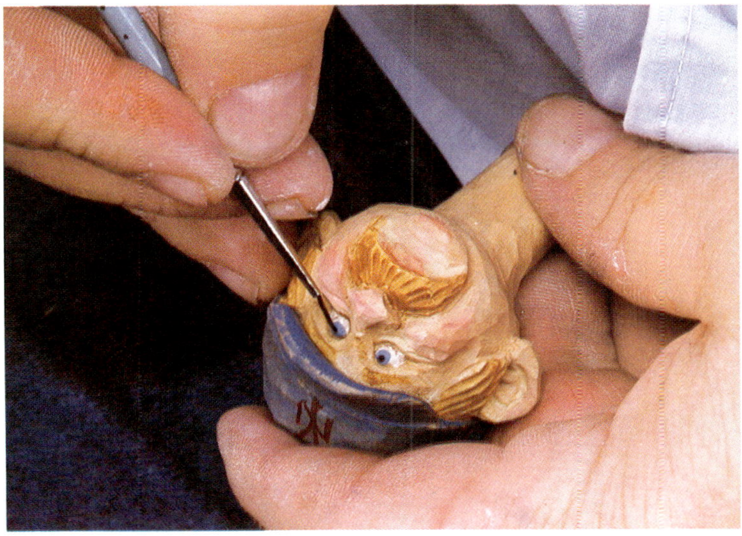

Paint a black pupil in the eye.

Add a dot of white to the eye to bring it to life.

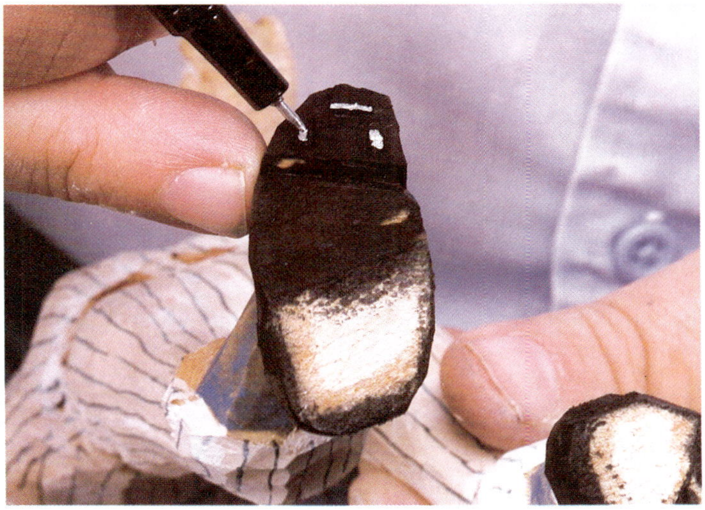

A pen with silver metallic ink makes the cleats look real.

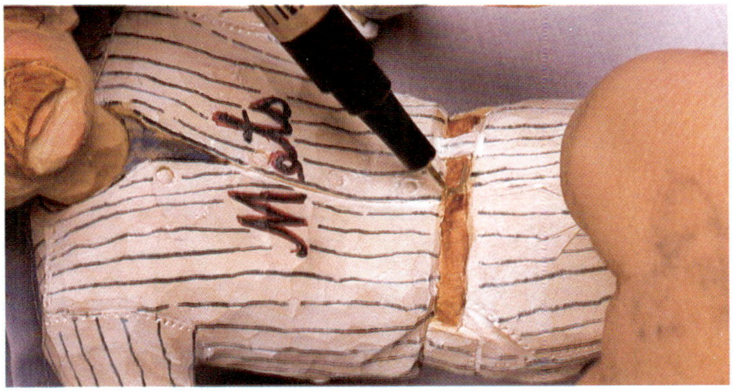

Another pen, with gold metallic ink, brings some sparkle to the belt buckle.

The finished pitcher.

The Gallery

"Casey," manager

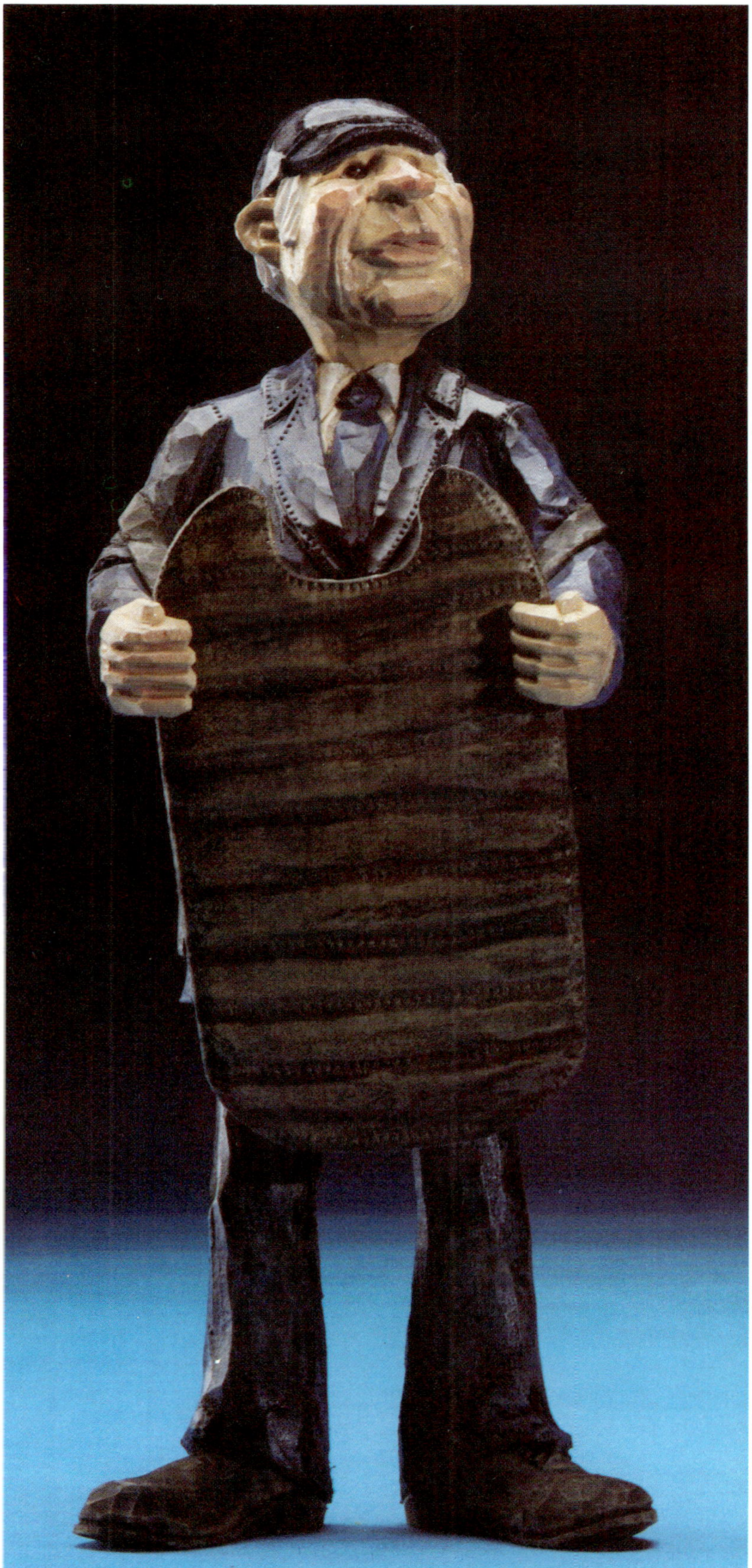

"Blind" Bart, umpire

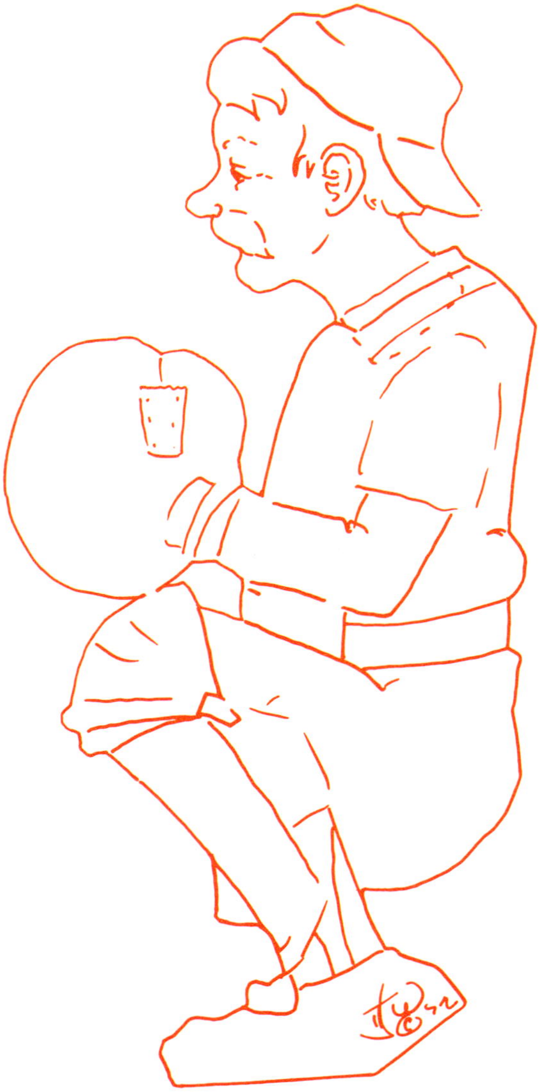

Billy "Butterfingers" Bailey, catcher

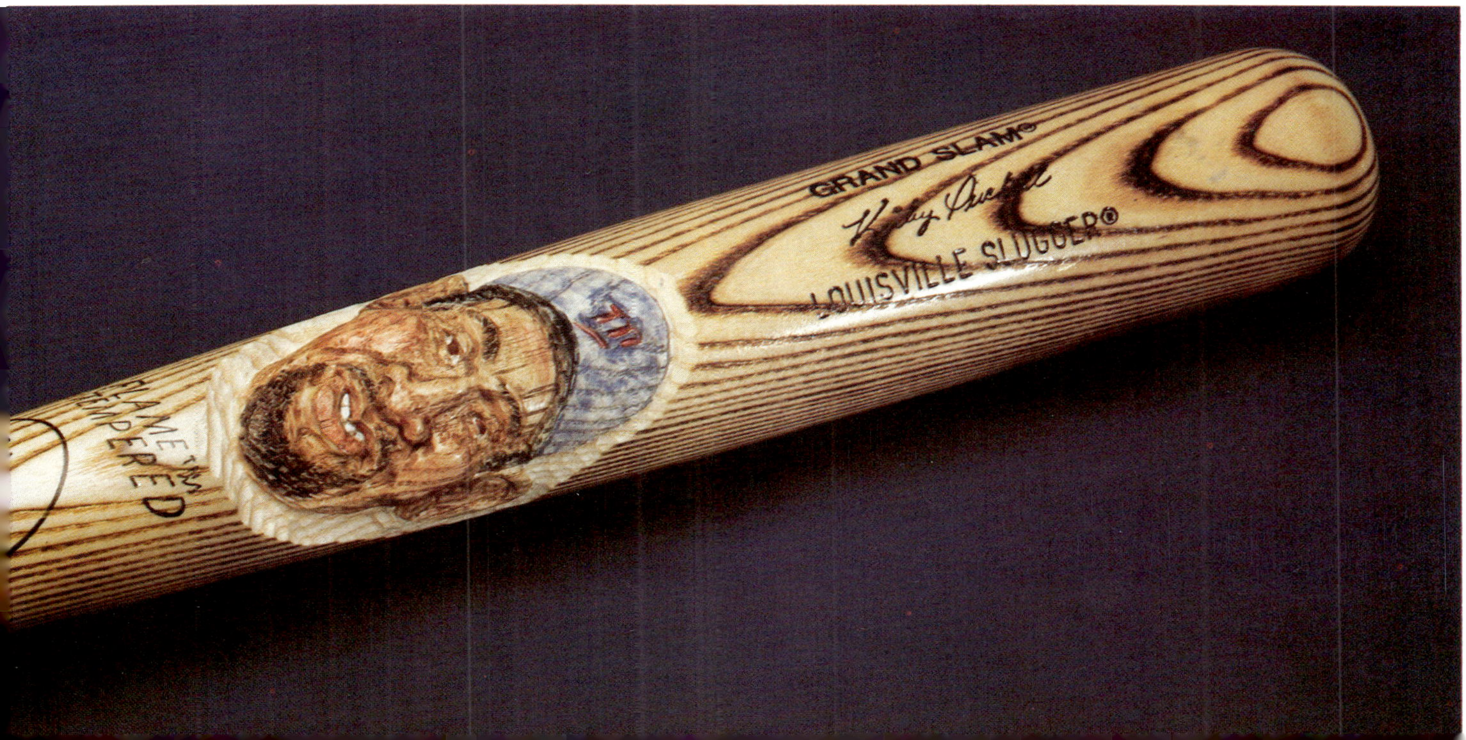

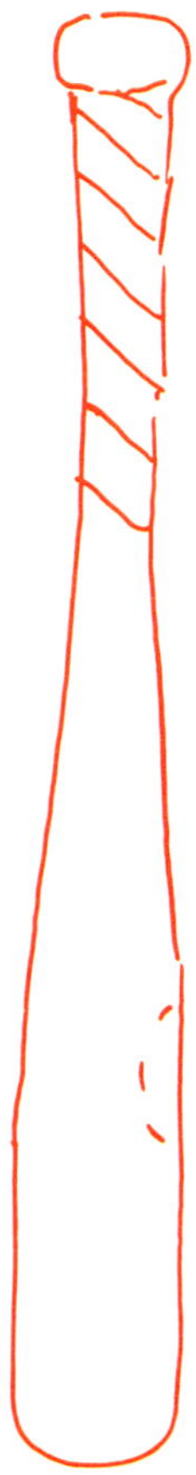

Pete "Pop-up" Rauscher

5

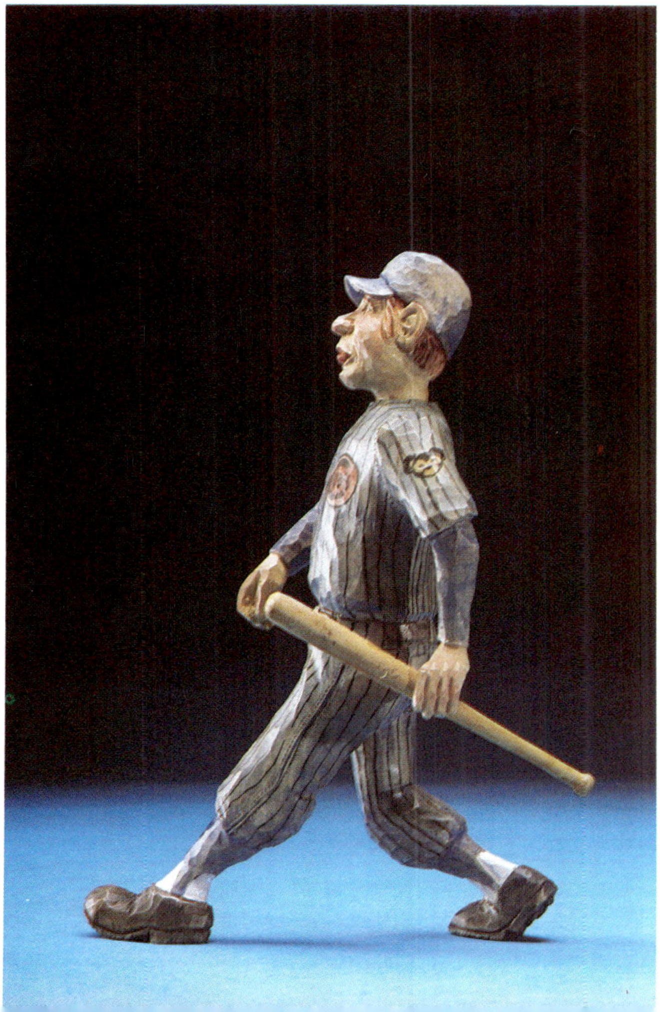

CUBS

Danny "Spitball" Marlow, pitcher

Left: Willy Wildthrow, 1st base & Right: Chief Lightfoot, 2nd base

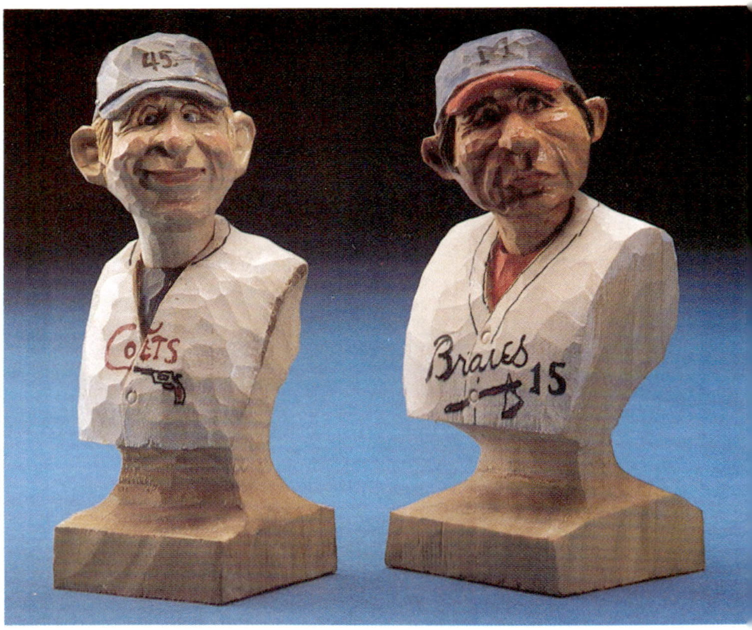

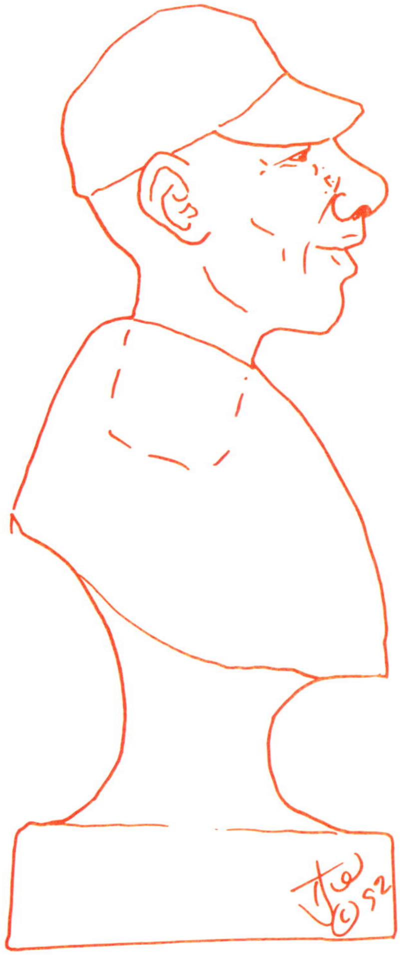

Left: Fast Freddy Fireball, shortstop & Right: Wilbur "Scratch" Wilson, 3rd base

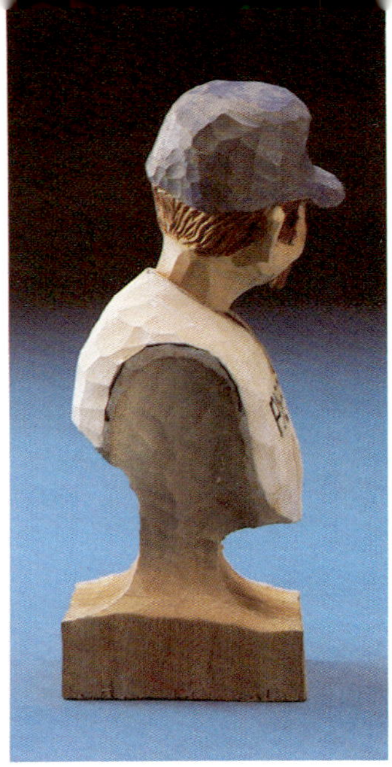

Left: Sleepy Sam Slaughter, Leftfield. Center: Lenny "Longarm" Lasser, Centerfield. Right: "Weakarm" Watson, Rightfield

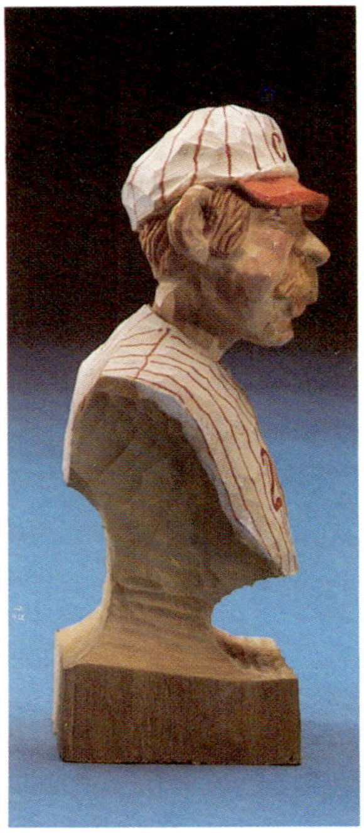